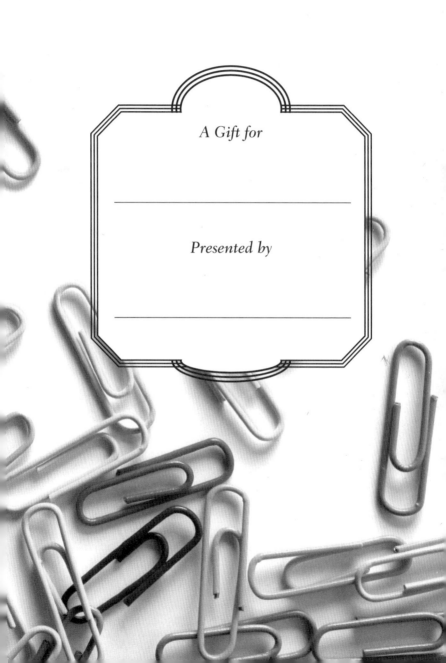

A Gift for

_____

Presented by

_____

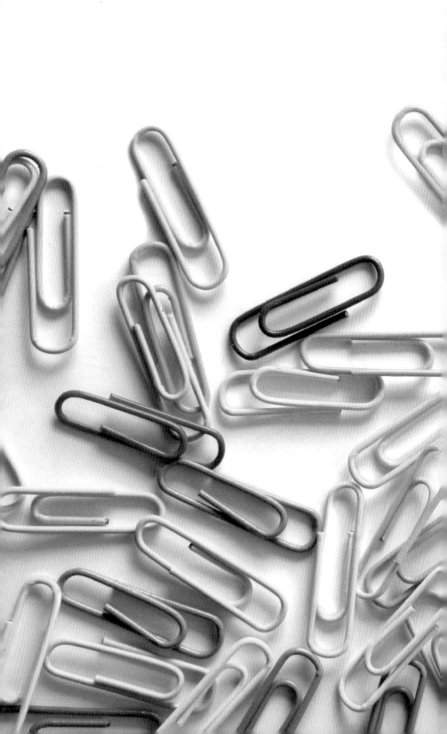

THE OFFICE BOOK

"I love deadlines.
I like the whooshing sound they
make as they fly by."

—*Douglas Adams,* author

THE OFFICE BOOK

Subversive Ways to Survive the 9-to-5 Grind

CHLOE RHODES

The Reader's Digest Association, Inc.
Pleasantville, New York/Montreal

A READER'S DIGEST BOOK

Copyright © 2010 Michael O'Mara Books Limited
All rights reserved. Unauthorized reproduction, in any manner, is prohibited.
Reader's Digest is a registered trademark of The Reader's Digest Association, Inc.
First published in Great Britain in 2009 by Michael O'Mara Books Limited,
    9 Lion Yard, Tremadoc Road, London SW4 7NQ

FOR READER'S DIGEST
U.S. Project Editor: Barbara Booth
Manager, English Book Editorial, Reader's Digest Canada: Pamela Johnson
Project Designer: Elizabeth Tunnicliffe
Senior Art Director: George McKeon
Executive Editor, Trade Publishing: Dolores York
Manufacturing Manager: Elizabeth Dinda
Associate Publisher, Trade Publishing: Rosanne McManus
President and Publisher, Trade Publishing: Harold Clarke

Library of Congress Cataloging-in-Publication Data
Rhodes, Chloe.
  The office book : subversive ways to survive the 9-to-5 grind / Chloe Rhodes.
      p. cm.
  "First published in Great Britain in 2009 by Michael O'Mara Books Limited."
  ISBN 978-1-60652-109-0
  1. Work--Humor. 2. Work--Anecdotes. 3. Office politics--Humor. 4. Office practice--
Humor. I. Title.
  PN6231.W644R47 2010
  818'.602--dc22

                                    2009051429

We are committed to both the quality of our products and the service we provide to our
customers. We value your comments, so please feel free to contact us:

    The Reader's Digest Association, Inc.
    Adult Trade Publishing
    Reader's Digest Road
    Pleasantville, NY 10570-7000

For more Reader's Digest products and information, visit our website:
    www.rd.com (in the United States)
    www.readersdigest.ca (in Canada)

Photography credits: Shutterstock Images; iStockphoto;
    The Reader's Digest Association, Inc./GID

Printed in the United States of America

1 3 5 7 9 10 8 6 4 2

ACKNOWLEDGMENTS
With thanks to Silvia Crompton, Lindsay Davies, and the numerous friends and
colleagues who shared their stories of office life, but who, in the interests of protecting
their jobs and in many cases their dignity, have asked to remain anonymous.

Contents

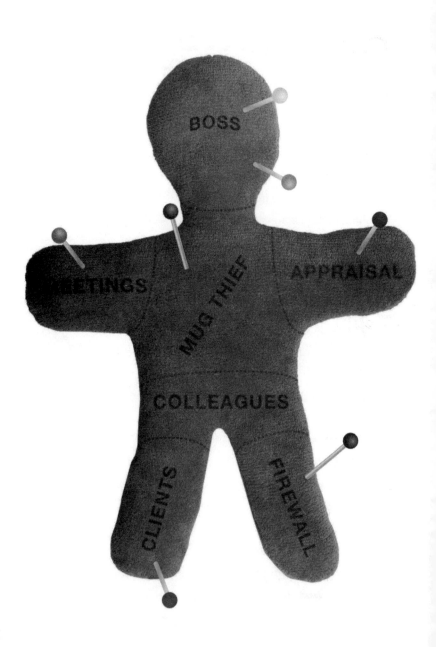

Office
Survival

"Nothing is really work unless you would rather be doing something else."

—*J. M. Barrie*

MONDAY morning, 7 o'clock. You're woken from a restful slumber by the high-pitched screech of your alarm. In the haze of the half-light, you're lost for a moment in the world of waking dreams. Perhaps you picture yourself rising slowly and plotting your day's activities over a bagel and freshly ground coffee in a sunlit café, at peace with the world and in control of your own destiny. You reach out blindly to switch on the lamp, and the grim reality hits you like a slap in the face: There is only one place you are going, and it's the same place you went to yesterday and the day before that. It's the same place, in fact, that you'll go to tomorrow, every day next week, and possibly for the next forty years of your life: the office.

During our careers, we spend almost 60,000 hours sitting at our office desks, where we write 50,000 to-do lists, receive more than 320,000 e-mails and drink 32,000 cups of coffee. Most of us spend more time at the office—an average of 8.2 hours per day—than we spend on any other aspect of our lives. For some of us, it becomes a strange sort of second home—the soothing whir of the photocopier, the rhythmic flicker of fluorescent lights, and the never-ending pattern of coffee-stained carpet tiles that weave themselves into the very fabric of our beings until life doesn't seem right unless we're swiveling on an ergonomic chair on wheels and speaking in Office Jargonese (see page 15).

The science of wasted time

Despite the epic number of hours we spend in the office, many of us are kept busy just killing time. Here are some facts and figures (well, this *is* an office book) showing the mind-rotting amount of wasted time clocked by the average office employee.

Time Spent... ## Doing What...

5.6 hours a week	sitting in meetings doodling ourselves to distraction
6 minutes a day	deleting e-mails that promise free Viagra, college degrees, and Nigerian bank accounts
10 hours a week	sending e-mails
27 minutes each lunch hour	waiting on line
50 times a day	checking inboxes
50 minutes a week	listening to brain-deadening music while on hold
64 minutes a day	venting about office politics

Meetings deemed to be utterly unproductive	**69 percent**
People who eat lunch *al desko,* presumably looking industrious while actually booking vacations or downloading music	**75 percent**

You may not be adding all this up, but in summary, most of us will waste a grand total of seventeen hours in an average forty-five-hour workweek.

Whistle while you work?

Enduring the life-sapping tedium of the office might be less of a challenge if we actually enjoyed what we did. Sadly, however, most of us do not. In fact, a soul-destroying average of 50 percent of people feel unfulfilled in their jobs. Now *there's* something the guidance counselor at school never mentioned.

Aaaaarrrrrrrrggggggghhhh!

Stress seems to top most people's lists of problems at work, with almost half of office employees suffering from it. Forty-one percent say the cause is the constant struggle to balance work and life, 38 percent attribute it to poor management, and 33 percent say it is a symptom of unachievable targets. But there is also evidence to suggest that simply being *in* the office might be to blame. You suspected it all along, right?

A global review of the impact of modern office design found that the move toward open-plan environments, with their echoing noise and lack of personal space, has had "shocking" effects on our physical and mental health. Ninety percent of those who had made the switch from private to open-plan office reported adverse effects, ranging from an increase in colds to anxiety and depression.

The one crumb of comfort for

despairing office denizens is that, on top of the financial outlay involved in creating an open-plan office in the first place, employers are losing billions in sick pay each year as the number of working days lost due to stress soars.

Chronic office overload syndrome

The office environment has an impact on every facet of our lives: our diets are dictated by the limited repertoire of the cafeteria chef or the office's proximity to a McDonald's. Our friendships are forged in accordance with office hierarchies, and our free time is structured by office-sanctioned annual leave. Our clothes are office clothes, our gossip is office gossip, even the air we breathe—recycled thirty-eight times through the bacteria-infested air-conditioning unit— is office air. Is it any wonder we struggle to survive in such stifling conditions?

Office workers of the world, unite! We have nothing to lose but our jobs.

The rules of office survival

We've already established that it's a cruel old world in there, but until our planet is taken over by some alien entity that has never heard of spreadsheets and thinks an appraisal is in some way linked to "praise," we must find a way to cope. Take these simple rules below as your starting point.

If at first you don't succeed, remove all evidence you ever tried.

If at first you *do* succeed, try not to look too startled.

You have to be 100 percent behind someone before you can stab them in the back.

Quitters never win; winners never quit. But those who never win and never quit are just idiots.

Don't play cat-and-mouse games if you have any reason to suspect that you might be the mouse.

If you can't do things correctly, at least be consistent.

When in doubt, nod your head slowly and smile a knowing smile.

Doing a job right the first time gets the job done. Doing the job wrong 14 times gives you job security.

When faced with a seemingly insurmountable problem, ask yourself: What would SpongeBob do?

Never underestimate the power of very stupid people in large groups.

It's only when you run out of options that the solution becomes clear.

If you're feeling despondent about spending your working life asleep at your desk, take a moment to consider how much worse it must be for insomniacs.

Conformity will get you promoted more quickly than competence.

If you arrive late, everyone will notice; if you leave late, nobody will notice.

Photocopiers can smell your fear.

If someone says, "Oh *here* he/she is!" when you enter a room, it's time to start browsing the job section.

Pride, commitment, and teamwork are words used to get you to work for free.

Never be too good at the tough jobs; you'll only be given more of them.

Don't make yourself irreplaceable; if they can't replace you, they won't promote you.

Jargonese

> "The stuff that was coming out of him consisted of words, but it was not speech in the true sense: it was a noise uttered in unconsciousness, like the quacking of a duck."
>
> —*George Orwell,* 1984

ONE of the most frustrating aspects of office life is the way it clutters our heads with embarrassing words and phrases that sound ridiculous and mean nothing. Most entries in the Jargonese dictionary sound like the kind of thing an eight-year-old would make up while playing at working in an office. (Which, if it happened, would be a tragic indictment of a society that believes work-obsessed office staff make acceptable role models for our children. But I digress.)

The worst thing of all, though, is the way these terms creep into the subconscious. All of us start off hating them. We mock the managers who seem incapable of stringing a sentence together without including the phrase "by end of day," and exchange withering glances when our so-called superiors tell us to "think outside the box."

But just when we least expect it, they burst forth like the alien erupting from John Hurt's chest and make you look like an imbecile. It can happen anywhere: You might be sitting in a bar with your friends or having Sunday lunch with your parents when suddenly a terrible silence descends and everyone stares at you as someone shrieks, "Did you just say that you want to 'touch base' to find out the plans for the weekend?" And the tragedy is that you did, you *actually* did.

So, depending on your level of exposure to jargonese, use this list either to interpret what is being said by your already brainwashed colleagues or to decontaminate your mind by learning which phrases you must never be heard to utter again.

Glossary of office jargon

Low-hanging fruit: Formerly described as a "quick win," this is a task that can be completed in a short space of time with a minimum amount of effort.

Flight risk: Someone who is suspected of leaving the department or company soon.

Looking under the hood: Getting to grips with a problem by investigating it at a deeper level, as a mechanic who actually has a skilled job might.

360-degree thinking: Er, thinking about something from all angles?

The golden thread: The characteristic that brings cohesion and uniformity to a project; sometimes also referred to as the "gold-plated thread" if said characteristic looks all right on the surface but is bound to wear thin if it rubs up against anything hard.

By end of day: By the end of the working day. Often used by middle managers who think that eliminating articles such as "the" and "an" make you appear more important.

Cleanup hitter: Someone who comes in to solve a problem or lead a team. In baseball the cleanup hitter's role is to clear the bases by driving other runners home to score runs. Used by middle managers who fantasize about the sports field.

Leveraging core competencies: Making the best possible use of the tiny list of things we can do well.

Cascade down: The trickle of policy or ideas from the top of an organization downward, in the manner of a waterfall—or perhaps a sewage system.

Strategic staircase: A detailed plan for the future. (Surely they've invented the evolutionary escalator by now?)

Blamestorming: Sitting around in a group discussing why a deadline was missed or a project failed and who screwed it up.

Cube farm: An office filled with cubicles.

Prairie-dogging: When something happens in a cube farm and everyone's head pops over their cubicle.

Let's stir-fry some ideas in the creativity wok: Oh, dear, it's too awful for words.

Blue-sky thinking: Thinking creatively. Generally used by people who can only come up with this one overused and painfully hackneyed way of putting into words the concept of thinking creatively.

Sunsetting the idea: Scrapping a plan that was probably never going to work in the first place.

I don't have enough bandwidth: I'm afraid I haven't the time or resources to acquiesce to your demands.

Idea hamsters: People who are good at generating new ideas—this is apparently linked in some mysterious way to the notion that the wheels hamsters use to exercise are like constantly whirring idea generators. (See what I mean about the eight-year-old?)

Tourists: Employees who take training sessions to get a free vacation.

Circling the drain: A project that is dying a slow death.

Say what?

If your manager says: **They really mean:**

Activate   Make copies and add more names to the memo

All-new   The system's not compatible with existing working practices

Approved, subject to comment   Redo the darn thing

Clarify   Fill in the background with so many details that the foreground goes underground

Confidential memorandum   No time to photocopy for the whole office

Consultant   Someone who borrows your watch to tell you what time it is, then walks away with the watch

Coordinator   The person who has a desk between two expediters

Expedite   To confound confusion with commotion

If your manager says:	They really mean:
Forwarded for your consideration	You hold the bag for a while
Give someone the picture	Make a long, confused, inaccurate statement to a newcomer
In due course	Never
It is in process	So wrapped up in red tape that the situation is almost hopeless
It's company policy	Just do it
Let's get together on this	I'm assuming you're as confused as I am
Note and initial	If this goes wrong, I need a watertight way of blaming you
Project	Any assignment that cannot be completed by one single telephone call
See me	Come down to my office; I'm lonely and scared

If your manager says:	They really mean:
Team player	Someone who's given up everything in his life, has no opinion whatsoever, and will never challenge upper management
Top priority	It's a stupid idea, but the head honcho wants it
Under consideration	I've lost the original memo
Will look into it	Please forget about it, please forget about it

Unofficial office jargon that works for you

The one advantage of all the pseudospeak that floods offices across the world is that it creates a blanket of vagueness beneath which all sorts of meanings can be concealed. If you want to be able to communicate with your colleagues without the boss knowing what you're talking about—or talk to your boss without him or her knowing what you're talking about—then why not turn the tables and use a bit of jargon of your own?

Seagull manager: A manager who flies in, makes lots of noise, craps all over everything, and flies off again

Interdepartmental liaison facilitation: Lunch with a colleague

Black-sky thinking: I'm thinking it's time to go home

Nonspecific interfacing: Idle chitchat

Flexing the hamstrings: Taking an extended lunch break

Downloading hardware: Using the bathroom

Uploading software: Stuffing one's face with a white-chocolate cranberry muffin

On standby: Staring into space

Dilberted: To be exploited and oppressed by your boss

"Notice me!" Memos from Mars

> "A memorandum is written not to inform
> the reader but to protect the writer."
>
> —*Dean Acheson*

YOU might think that the old-fashioned act of writing a notice and sticking it onto a corkboard would give people time—in a way that sending e-mails does not—to think carefully about what they want to say and how to say it. Giving your note a quick read-through before plastering it up for all to see seems the least you could do. But, perhaps not surprisingly, the office environment is not conducive to a moment's quiet reflection, and so our walls and corkboards are pockmarked with memos that make their authors sound uptight, dyslexic, eccentric or completely deranged.

The following pages contain a collection of worryingly real examples.

LIGHTING:

Just a reminder, the spotlights on the posters are only for use during client visits. Do not use more lighting than is necessary, as usage of excess lighting increases our "carbon footprint."

!!DANGER!!
THE HOT WATER
HEATS UP VERY
QUICKLY
—IT'S SO HOT
IT'S NOT FUNNY.

PLEASE
APPROACH THE
WATERCOOLER
ONE PERSON
AT A TIME!

SCENT-FREE DETERGENT:

Just a reminder for everyone that as the seasons change, allergies are even more sensitive to simple triggers. Please make sure you are using a scent-free detergent on the laundry you wear into the office.

PLEASE NOTE:

In the interests of creating a pleasant working atmosphere, please could all staff take a shower at least three times a week–using shampoo and shower gel.

The Boss..

There will be a turkey shoot at today's company picnic, in the rear.

TOILET OUT OF ORDER. PLEASE USE FLOOR BELOW.

Would the person who took the step-ladder yesterday please bring it back or further steps will be taken.

And, of course, those wonderful e-mails containing gobbledegook that come from the IT department:

Attention: All Staff Who Use CYIM, Site Contacts, LAN Administrators:

CYIM Release 6.17 will be implemented on Sunday September 28, 2008. The key change to CYIM in this release is the ability to access the new Detailed Assessment Record (DAR) and the Ongoing Case Assessment Record (OCAR) for Champion Sites. For detailed information on this CYIM enhancement please visit: ACS Worklinks> Tools > Work Information Module>Release Notes>CYIM Release 6.17 Document

Please note: Scheduled downtime to implement CYIM Release 6.17 will be on Sunday September 28, 2008 from 7 A.M. to 11 A.M. Please note that CYIM will not be available during this time. The new Release will be available for use at 11 A.M. on Sunday September 28, 2008. It is essential that all staff are logged off CYIM before 7 A.M. on Sunday September 28, 2008. We can not apply the release to your worksite if any workstation is still logged into CYIM.

When you log into CYIM after 11 A.M. on Sunday September 28, 2008 access the UTILITIES MENU and select DISPLAY APPLICATION VERSION to ensure you are running Application Version 6.17. Note To LAN Administrators: Please leave the File Server up and running to allow Release 6.17 to be implemented at your site.

If you have any questions or require additional information please contact Applications (CYIM) Support. Thank you.

> **HEATING ISSUES:**
> I have been advised by the building operators that they have turned off the air-conditioning for the entire building so it should get warmer on all of our floors. If you do get too warm, please let me know so that I can advise them. Also, I believe there is a problem with hot water in the building, as in there is none. They are working on that problem as well.
> Thanks

> THESE CUPBOARDS ARE FOR THE STORAGE OF OFFICE EQUIPMENT ONLY—PLEASE DO NOT USE THEM FOR STORING VALUABLES, GYM KITS OR 18 PAIRS OF SHOES.

Pest control

We are working hard to combat the mouse problem but our efforts will be wasted unless staff makes sure that no food is left in the office unless it is properly stored. We have provided Tupperware containers for this purpose. Mice have been found in drawers and inside filing cabinets so just because the food is out of sight, it isn't out of mind. Thank you.

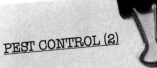

PEST CONTROL (2)

Please ensure that the floor space beneath your desks is left clear this weekend as chemicals will be sprayed to tackle the flea problem. The flea problem would be solved by getting rid of the mice, which will only be possible if staff makes sure that no food is left in the office unless it is properly stored. We have provided Tupperware containers for this purpose. Mice have been found in drawers and inside filing cabinets so just because the food is out of sight, it isn't out of mind. Thank you.

GARBAGE: for several months the desk next to the recycling bins has been vacant and the extra space has been used as an overflow area for the garbage cans. Please note that there is now someone trying to work at that desk three days a week so do not leave your garbage all over it, even if it looks as though there's no one there.

This firm requires no physical-fitness program. Everyone gets enough exercise jumping to conclusions, flying off the handle, running down the boss, knifing coworkers in the back, dodging responsibility, and pushing their luck.

* * * * * * * * * * * * * * * * *

If you are in the bathroom longer than 15 minutes, it will be considered a break. Don't make us get a timer!

MANAGEMENT

* * * * * * * * * * * * * * * * *

HELLO,
There is leftover chicken curry in the 7th Floor lunchroom from Joel's Seminar. Please go very quietly; the seminar is still in session.

Résumé Nightmares

> "If all else fails, immortality can always
> be assured by spectacular error."
>
> —*John Kenneth Galbraith*

A H, résumés: so boring and yet so vital—and, more often than not, so full of crap that our own mothers wouldn't recognize us from them. They're an open invitation to exaggerate, and we willingly oblige, from the odd "white lie" that mildly overemphasizes our leadership experience to the barefaced fabrications that portray us as championship horse jumpers with triple-firsts and a knack for busting scientology spy rings. And if we're not making ourselves look unrealistically good, we're making ourselves look all too believably stupid with deal-breaking typos and shocking personal revelations.

The recent craze for video résumés, sent as electronic links to YouTube or MySpace in the sadly mistaken belief that they will be the best showcase for a candidate's "skills," has increased the potential for humiliation a hundredfold. The first disaster hit the Web in 2006, when a Yale University student submitted his six-minute, forty-three-second video entitled "Impossible is Nothing"—accompanied by photos and an eleven-page résumé—to a Wall Street investment firm. In the film, the student describes his attitude toward success and demonstrates his sporting prowess with performances in weightlifting, tennis, skiing and ballroom dancing. You can perhaps imagine how that went down with the recruitment board.

But at least the recruiters had been entertained. Human Resources managers the world over have a love-hate relationship with résumés. On the one hand, they can be coma-inducing nightmares—one recruiter fondly remembers the candidate who sent in a nine-page cover letter accompanied by a four-page résumé—but on the other hand, they can be catastrophically and unintentionally hilarious. The following excerpts come from real résumés that have been submitted for real jobs (though, fortunately, not all from the same person).

Personal details

Age: "Although I'm sixty-two I'm as fit as a
forty-nine-year-old."

Marital Status: "Often."

Children: "Various."

Marital status: "Single. Unmarried. Uninvolved.
No commitments."

Marital status: "Not known."

Sex: "Occasionally."

Emergency contact number: "911."

Number of dependents: "40."

"I limit important relationships to people who want
to do what I want them to do."

"My family is willing to relocate. However, not to
New England (too cold) and not to southern California
(earthquakes). Indianapolis or Chicago would be fine. My
youngest prefers Orlando's proximity to Disney World."

Education

"Twin sister has accounting degree."

"Finished eighth in my class of ten."

"Failed bar exam with relatively high grades."

"I've got a Ph.D. in human feelings."

Education: "College, August 1880–May 1984."

"I am about to enrol on a Business and Finance Degree with the Open University. I feel that this qualification will prove detrimental to me for future success."

"I possess a moderate educatin but willing to learn more."

"Have repeated courses repeatedly."

Educational background: "High school was a incredible experience."

"My father is a computer programmer, so I have 15 years of computer experience."

Skills

"Bleaching, pot washing, window cleaning, mopping, etc."

"Strong Work Ethic, Attention to Detail, Team Player, Self Motivated, Attention to Detail."

"I have lurnt Word Perfect 6.0 computor and spreasheet progroms."

"Able to say the ABC's backward in under five seconds."

"Am a perfectionist and rarely if if ever forget details."

"I can type without looking at thekeyboard."

"My contributions on product launches were based on dreams that I had."

"I am loyal to my employer at all costs... Please feel free to respond to my resume on my office voice mail."

"It's best for employers that I not work with people."

"I procrastinate, especially when the task is unpleasant."

"Can function without additional oxygen at
   24,000 feet."

"I have integrity so I will not steal office supplies
   and take them home."

"I have technical skills that will take your
   breath away."

"Have not yet been abducted by aliens."

"Written communication = 3 years; verbal
   communication = 5 years."

"I bring doughnuts on Friday."

"National record for eating 45 eggs in two minutes."

"I have a lifetime's worth of technical expertise
   (I wasn't born—my mother simply chose 'eject child'
   from the special menu)."

"I am bilingual in three languages."

Previous Experience

"Wholly responsible for two (2) failed financial institutions."

"I'm a hard worker, etc."

"I was working for my mother until she moved without telling me."

"1990–1997: Stewardess—U.S. Air Force."

"Service for old man to check they are still alive or not."

"Planned new corporate facility at $3 million over budget."

"Brought in a balloon artist to entertain the team."

"I have extensive experience with foreign accents."

"28 dog years of experience in sales (four human)."

Interests

"The sea in all its forms."

"Running, editing video, cooking, writing and wondering."

"Getting drunk every night down by the water, playing my guitar and smoking pot."

"Having a good time."

"Gossiping."

"Donating blood. Fourteen gallons so far!"

"Playing with my two dogs (they actually belong to my wife but I love the dogs more than my wife)."

"Stalking, shipping and receiving."

"Sitting on the levee at night watching alligators."

"Playing trivia games. I am a repository of worthless knowledge."

"Mushroom hunting."

Reason for leaving previous employment

"My boss thought I could do better elsewhere."

"I thought the world was coming to an end."

"They insisted all employees get to work by 8:45 A.M. every morning. I couldn't work under those conditions."

"The company made me a scapegoat, just like my three previous employers."

"Note: Please don't misconstrue my 14 jobs as 'job-hopping.' I have never quit a job."

"Responsibility makes me nervous."

"Was met with a string of broken promises and lies, as well as cockroaches."

"I need money because I have bills to pay and I would like to have a life, go out partying, please my young wife with gifts, and have a menu entrée consisting of more than soup."

"Starting over due to recent bankruptcies. Need large bonus when starting job."

"Pushed aside so the vice president's girlfriend could steal my job."

"Terminated after saying, "It would be a blessing to be fired.'"

"We stole a pig, but it was a really small pig."

References

"None. I've left a path of destruction behind me."

"Bill, Tom, Eric. But I don't know their phone numbers."

Call That a Cover Letter?

"Avoid employing unlucky people:
throw half of the pile of résumés in the
bin without reading them."

—*David Brent,* The Office

As if the résumé itself didn't present enough possibilities for sounding like an idiot, the cover letter is a full page of white space just begging to be filled with self-aggrandizing clichés or desperate pleas to be given just one little break.

We've all been taught the official way to compose these things—put a bit about why you want the job and a bit about why you're suited to it, etc., etc.—and yet so often we let ourselves deviate from the path that wiser job seekers have laid down for us. We want to stand out from the crowd, we want to wow them with our wit and insight, we want, above all, to be loved, even by managers we'll soon come to loathe.

And so we spin our webs of deceit, littering our all-important letters with typing errors and spelling mistakes in our rush to prove how brilliant we are, with spectacular results.

The bold

"Let's meet, so you can "ooh" and "ahh" over my experience."

"Brainstorming on innovative ideas that take into consideration demographics, target markets, advertising strategies, and shifts in the economy that have a direct impact on consumer buying trends and the influences that drive those changes is one of my other strengths."

"I am a dilettante and a factotum whose knowledge of English and its usage, earmark me as an ideal candidate."

"My name is J— F—, and I kick ass. See resume for details."

The ambitious

"Although I trained as an accountant and for the past eight years I worked for a major accountancy firm, I am no good at my job and get bored very easily.

So I'm looking for something different and wondered if you have any other opportunities that may be of interest to me?"

"My goal is to be a meteorologist. But since I possess no training in meteorology, I suppose I should try stock brokerage."

"My ultimate goal is to become a doctor, but since I was not able to get into medical school I would like to work for your company."

"You will want me to be Head Honcho in no time."

The demanding

"Hi, i attached my resume please look it over and give me a call thank you."

"I am forwarding my resume to you for your review. Please look this over and hire me for any type of work you have available."

"So one of the main things for me is, as the movie *Jerry McGuire* puts it, 'Show me the money!'"

The honest

"For the last twelve years I have been involved in gang crime including burglary, drug dealing, extortion, armed robbery and internet scams. With this inside knowledge I would make an ideal policeman."

"I can be pretty energetic and chatty when I'm not demonstrating the wisdom behind the old saying that 'tis better to be silent and be presumed a fool than to speak and remove all doubt."

"I am very bad about time and don't mind admitting it. Having to arrive at a certain hour doesn't make sense to me. What does make sense is that I do the job. Any company that insists upon rigid time schedules will find me a nightmare."

"Don't take the comments of my former employers too seriously. They don't know what they are talking about."

The impassioned

"I read through the posting with great excitement for two reasons; one being that the coffee served up at Café Ritazza is quality drip."

"I am a man filled with passion and integrity, and I can act on short notice. I'm a class act and do not come cheap."

The unhinged

"I am a wedge with a sponge taped to it. My purpose is to wedge myself into someone's door to absorb as much as possible."

"But no matter how we communicate to each other, whether by newspaper or Web site, the reliance on the use of words will always remain."

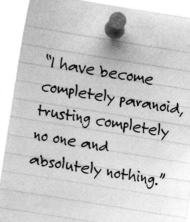

"I have become completely paranoid, trusting completely no one and absolutely nothing."

"I give a lot at all my jobs and that's when my soul is out in the ethers."

The world's greatest cover letter?

Sarah Beebe
23 Charles St.
Boston, Massachusetts

Dear Sarah,

I am writing in response to your advertisement in the ████████ newspaper on Monday, May 18.

I am a graduate who has recently returned from a round-the-world adventure and am excited to start a career in the television industry.

I believe I would be a suitable candidate for the position of receptionist, as I am a dynamic figure, often seen scaling walls and crushing ice. I write award-winning musicals, manage time efficiently, and occasionally tread water for three days in a row. I can ride bicycles up severe inclines with unflagging speed, can cook 30-minute brownies in 20 minutes, and am often seen ballooning across the Charles River on my lunch hour. I am expert in Portuguese, enjoy bungee jumping, and grow prizewinning green vegetables. Using only a hoe and a large glass of water, I once single-handedly defended a small village in the Amazon Basin from a horde of ferocious army ants. I am an abstract artist, a business analyst, and a ruthless bookie. Critics worldwide swoon over my original line of corduroy eveningwear. I don't perspire. I once read War and Peace, Moby Dick, and David Copperfield in one day and still had time to refurbish an entire dining room that evening. I know the exact location of every food item in the supermarket and have performed several covert operations with the CIA. I sleep once a week. While on vacation in Canada, I successfully negotiated with a group of terrorists who had seized a small bakery. The laws of physics don't apply to me. All my bills are paid. Years ago I discovered the meaning of life but forgot to write it down. I have won cliff-diving competitions in Sri Lanka, chess matches in the Kremlin, and full-contact origami in Japan. I have played Hamlet, I have performed open-heart surgery, and I have spoken with Elvis. But I have not yet worked in television.

I have enclosed my résumé for your information and would be happy to meet with you for an interview. I can be contacted at the above address and look forward to hearing from you.

Yours truly,

Barbara Taylor

The Dreaded Appraisal

"Judge me all you want, but keep the
verdict to yourself."

—Anonymous

YOU can imagine why, in the days before there
were appraisals, somebody thought having them
would be a good idea. In theory they sound as if they
could be productive, informative and supportive, giving us
all the opportunity to get a pat on the back for the things
we'd done well and some constructive criticism in the
areas in which we were found to be lacking. Perhaps they
were envisaged as a sort of comforting extension of the
school report, where we could be compensated for getting
a low grade by being given a gold star for effort and
guided toward promotion with challenging but achievable
targets for improvement. But as with all great utopian
dreams, the vision soon soured.

The annual appraisal is now very often just a frosty five
minutes in a drafty conference room in which both

participants try to avoid eye contact. The feedback is almost always negative, and the whole exercise seems like a management-sanctioned opportunity for senior members of staff to make paranoid digs about the lack of motivation evident in their underlings.

And so they developed the "360-degree appraisal—" which in English means the chance to give your boss feedback on what they're like to work for; how they might improve, say, their communication skills; or how they might tackle their habit of bullying the newest member of the team for the sheer hell of it. Right, like *that* would be a good career move....

Credit where credit's due

If your boss is of the breed that takes pleasure in watching you suffer—or you're just plain bad at your job—you might get feedback along the following lines:

"A prime candidate for natural deselection."

"A room-temperature IQ."

"Got a full six-pack, but lacks the plastic thingy to hold it all together."

"If brains were taxed, he'd get a rebate."

"If he were any more stupid, he'd have to be watered twice a week."

"The wheel is turning, but the hamster is dead."

"He has carried out each and every one of his duties to his entire satisfaction."

"This young lady has delusions of adequacy."

"This medical officer has used my ship to carry his genitals from port to port, and my officers to carry him from bar to bar."

"She sets low personal standards and then consistently fails to achieve them."

"He has the wisdom of youth and the energy of old age."

"Works well when under constant supervision and cornered like a rat in a trap.'"

"This man is depriving a village somewhere of an idiot."

"He brings a lot of joy whenever he leaves the room."

"When she opens her mouth, it seems it is only to change feet."

"This employee should go far, and the sooner the better."

"A gross ignoramus: 144 times worse than an ordinary ignoramus."

"When his IQ reaches 50, he should sell."

"If you see two people talking and one looks bored, he's the other one."

"A photographic memory, but with the lens cover glued on."

"Donated his brain to science before he was done using it."

"If you stand close enough to him, you can hear the ocean."

"It's hard to believe that he beat 1,000,000 other sperm."

"One neuron short of a synapse."

"Some drink from the fountain of knowledge,
  he only gargled."

Appraisal jargon

If, on the other hand, you have a boss who knows you'll
see the outcome of their appraisal of you before you
complete yours of them, you might get comments that
need a bit of decoding:

If your boss writes:	It really means:
Exceptionally well qualified	Has committed no major mistakes to date
Active socially	Drinks heavily
Zealous attitude	Opinionated
Character above reproach	Still one step ahead of the law
Quick-thinking	Offers plausible excuses for errors
Takes pride in his work	Conceited
A sharp analyst	Thoroughly confused

If your boss writes:	It really means:
Takes advantage of every opportunity to progress	Buys drinks for superiors
Forceful	Argumentative and aggressive
Expresses himself well	Speaks English
Conscientious and careful	Scared
Meticulous in attention to detail	Incredibly anal
Demonstrates qualities of leadership	Has a loud voice
Excellent sense of humor	Has a vast repertoire of dirty jokes
Loyal	Can't get another job elsewhere
Stern disciplinarian	A drill sergeant
Relaxed attitude	Sleeps on the desk

Interview Awkwardness

Office rule #1: The clammier your hand, the drier the hand of the person with whom you shake hands with.

IT is one of the many sad ironies of office life that the one thing that keeps us in the jobs we hate is our failure to secure a new job in a different office that we would hate just as much. Still, without hope we have nothing, so we must go on believing that somewhere out there is an office with cheerful, contented employees, a TV room with enormous sofas, inspiring bosses and cozy sleeping compartments for mid-afternoon naps.

And in order to follow that dream, we have to go on attending interviews and, ideally, getting job offers— something recent research suggests we're pathetically bad at. Despite arming ourselves with charms, mascots and lucky underwear, surveys indicate that workers miss out on billions of dollars' worth of pay raises each year through unsuccessful interviews, and one in three people seeking a new position fail to receive a single job offer in the space of a year because of nerves or a poor interview technique.

But just how wrong can an interview go? Catastrophically wrong, apparently. Annual surveys of recruitment professionals and hiring managers reveal the full and comical extent of our interview incompetence. The following examples are real faux pas made by real applicants.

I knew a candidate who...

Told the interviewer he wouldn't be able to stay with the job long because he thought he might get an inheritance if his uncle died and that his uncle was "not looking too good."

Answered a personal phone call and asked the interviewer to leave her own office because it was a "private" conversation.

Wiped his nose with his hand repeatedly throughout the interview and then offered it to the interviewer to shake as he left.

Dabbed sweat off his forehead using his tie.

Brought her mother to the interview.

Asked the interviewer for a ride home.

Sniffed his armpits on the way into the interview room.

Said she could not provide a writing sample because all of her writing had been for the CIA and was "classified."

Told the interviewer that he was fired for beating up his last boss.

Turned down an offer of lunch before an interview, saying he didn't want to line his stomach with grease before going out drinking.

Applied for an accounting position and said she was a "people person" not a "numbers person."

Flushed the toilet during a telephone interview.

Took out a hairbrush in the middle of the interview and brushed her hair.

Claimed to be so well qualified that, if he didn't get the job, it would prove the company's management was incompetent.

Got off his chair and stretched out on the floor to fill out the job application.

Brought a large dog to the interview.

Chewed bubblegum and constantly blew bubbles as she answered questions.

Wore earphones attached to an MP3 player and claimed she could listen to the interviewer and the music at the same time.

Abruptly excused himself and returned to the office a few minutes later with his previously bald head covered by a hairpiece.

Challenged the interviewer to an arm wrestle.

Asked to see the interviewer's résumé to see if the personnel executive was qualified to interview him.

Announced she hadn't had lunch and proceeded to eat a hamburger and fries during the interview.

Asked the interviewer if he would put on a suit jacket to ensure the offer was formal.

Interrupted the interview to phone her therapist for advice on answering specific questions.

Told the interviewer that, if he were hired, he would demonstrate his loyalty by having the corporate logo tattooed on his forearm.

Refused to get out of his chair until the interviewer agreed to hire him. The interviewer eventually had to call the police to have him removed.

Stood up and started tap dancing around the interviewer's office when asked about his hobbies.

Brought with him a miniature pinball game and challenged the interviewer to play with him.

Bounced up and down on the office carpet and told the interviewer she must be highly thought of by the company to get such a thick carpet.

Pulled out a cell phone camera and snapped a picture of the interviewer. He claimed to collect photos of everyone who interviewed him.

Said he wasn't interested, because the job paid too much.

Took a ringing alarm clock out of his briefcase, shut it off, apologized, and said he had to leave for another interview.

Took out a copy of a popular men's magazine while the interviewer was in the middle of a long distance call and looked at the photos only, stopping longest at the centerfold.

Answered his phone during the interview and had a side conversation that went as follows: "Which company?...When do I start?...What's the salary?" When he hung up, the interviewer asked the applicant if he was still interested in completing the interview. To that he promptly responded, "I am as long as you'll pay me more." The interviewer did not hire him, and later found out there was no other job—it was a scam to get a better offer.

Arrived wearing only one shoe and explained the other was stolen off her foot on the bus.

Fumbled with his briefcase, which opened to reveal women's undergarments and assorted makeup and perfume.

Came to the interview on a moped and left it in the reception area. He didn't want it to get stolen, and announced he would require indoor parking for the moped if he were hired. He wasn't.

Removed his right shoe and sock and dusted the sole of his foot and the inside of the shoe with medicated foot powder. While he was putting the shoe and sock back on, he mentioned he had to use the powder four times a day and that this was the designated time.

Whistled while the interviewer was talking.

Asked who the "lovely babe" in the picture was and asked for the interviewer's home number when told it was his wife.

Threw up on the interviewer's desk and immediately started asking questions about the job, as if nothing had happened.

Sat down with his feet on the interviewer's desk and proceeded to tell her why he should have her job.

Pointed to a black case he'd carried into the interviewer's office and stated that, if he were not hired, the bomb would go off. Disbelieving, the interviewer began to explain why the applicant would never be hired and that he was going to call the police. The applicant then reached down to the case, flipped a switch, and ran. No one was injured, but the interviewer did need a new desk.

Started doing a tarot reading on the interviewer to check if they were compatible.

Insisted the interview be conducted in his car since he'd lost the keys and was worried about leaving it unattended.

Asked to be interviewed by the interviewer's superior instead.

Failed to notice until after the interview that her already-rather-mini skirt was tucked into her underpants.

Brought a bottle of chilled Champagne to the interview to celebrate the job offer he assumed would be forthcoming. It was not.

When interviewers turn bad

But laugh as they might at the level of our ineptitude, interviewers themselves are not without fault. As our school guidance counselors once so confidently reminded us, the interview is a two-way process—it's just as important for them to make the right impression on you as it is for you to wow them into offering you the job.

Top 15 interview warning signs

1. Two members of your interview panel clearly hate each other.

2. Two members of your interview panel clearly love each other.

3. They ask you to tell them a secret you've never told anyone else.

4. The interview is conducted in a windowless room.

5. The word "passion" is used in reference to planning spreadsheets.

6. The interviewer is sweating more than you are.

7. You're asked if you would ever break the law if your job demanded it.

8. You're asked if you would ever sleep with a client if your job demanded it.

9. You suspect that the person interviewing you is on hallucinogenic drugs.

10. Your interviewer breaks off mid-sentence and hums the theme song to *Big Brother*.

11. The interviewer asks you out on a date.

12. You have previously been on a date with the interviewer.

13. Your interviewer says, "And now we'll move on to the swimwear round."

14. You are ordered to make the interviewer's coffee and pick up her dry-cleaning before beginning the interview.

15. You are asked what you love most about meetings.

When interviewers get it wrong, they really get it wrong:

"In a telephone interview I had for a customer-service job, the woman interviewing me asked me to hold the line for a moment. I agreed and then listened as she muffled the receiver and had a whispered argument with someone called Mark in which she called him 'a pathetic muppet.'"

"I once had an interview in which I was asked if I were wearing tights."

"I went for a job as an admin assistant at an actors' agency, and the main agent walked into the interview room backward shouting to the staff outside the room, 'Who's the daddy? Who's the daddy?'"

"My interviewer ate a packet of sushi during our interview and, when it was finished, said, 'I love sushi but it does make your fingers smell of fish.'"

Reply All

"One of the symptoms of approaching nervous
breakdown is the belief that one's work is
terribly important. If I were a medical man,
I should prescribe a holiday to any patient
who considered his work important."

—*Bertrand Russell*

THERE can be no invention more likely to get us
into trouble in the office than e-mail. It's too easy,
too accessible and too tempting to be a safe method of
communication in a professional environment. And
research backs up the theory that it's doing us nothing
but harm. A study entitled "Trust and Risk in the
Workplace" looked at the computer habits of office
workers in the United States, Britain, Holland, and
Singapore and found that, on average, 34 percent of us
use e-mail to spread office gossip.

But rather than relishing the opportunity for a bit
of electronic chitchat, most of us find that sending
and receiving e-mails increases our stress levels. A
third of the population said that the sheer number of
e-mails they received made them feel stressed. The
amount of time taken up by managing this influx of

messages can also reach shocking proportions, with senior-management workers saying they spend an average of four hours a day just keeping up to date with their inboxes.

And the compulsive urge to check for new messages takes up even more time. Despite academics advising that we limit the number of times we check our inboxes in order to reduce stress levels, most workers who spend all day manacled to a computer switched applications to view their e-mail between thirty and forty times per hour. Perhaps more worrying still is the fact that we barely even register the notion that we're doing it; the participants of the study reported that they check their e-mails about once every fifteen minutes, but monitoring revealed that some of them were actually doing it ten times as often as they thought.

This intense level of distraction could be behind the vast number of e-mail blunders that occur every day.

The same scientists found that the constant breaking off of tasks in order to check e-mails made people's brains tired, which made them less productive and more prone to error. Incredibly, employees who were repeatedly distracted by their e-mails experienced a drop in IQ of ten points as a result. It's little wonder, then, that forty-two e-mail blunders happen every minute of every day.

Superpowered slip-up

You would think the Pentagon would be one of the few offices in the world guaranteed to come equipped with some sort of high-tech, anti-e-mail–catastrophe device. However, the office in which top military types devise highly confidential plans for the future of the planet is apparently at the whim of the same cruel fate as the rest of us.

A schoolgirl across the Atlantic in Devon, England, was innocently checking her e-mails one evening and found several messages containing top-secret information direct from the Pentagon. Her address had inexplicably been added to a classified e-mail list by a hapless navy commander.

The girl in question told reporters that she was particularly amused by one e-mail offering advice from the United States to the United Kingdom on how to prevent official secrets from being leaked.

Me, me, me!

Everyone wants to feel special on their twenty-first
birthday, but Citigroup employee Lucy Gao took self-
importance to a whole new level in an e-mail detailing the
arrangements for her party. The missive sounded more like
an A-list rock star's rider to his contract than an invitation
and featured a list of demands that the birthday girl
insisted her thirty-nine guests adhere to.

The e-mail ordered guests to contact Lucy through her
personal assistant "between 8:30 P.M. and 10:00 P.M."
if they had any questions, and divided the invitees into
groups, each with its own specified arrival time at
London's Ritz Hotel. Guests were encouraged to dress
"upper class" (no "bad taste") and were told in no
uncertain terms that Ms Gao would be "accepting cards
and small gifts between 9:00 P.M. and 11:00 P.M."

Although the birthday girl later insisted the whole thing
had been intended as a joke, the temptation evidently
proved too much for one bemused invitee, who started the
e-mail off on its global journey.

Firing blanks

The entire U.S. State Department's e-mail system once
crashed when a blank e-mail was sent to thousands of
employees on a global address list. Diplomats from all
over the world wrote back, either to demand to be
removed from the list or to complain about the mass

e-mailing of a blank message, but so many of them pressed "Reply all" that the whole system began to falter. Officials said that the problem was compounded when many of the flustered diplomats tried to recall their original responses (realizing perhaps that they had just committed the exact offense they were complaining about), which served only to generate yet another round of mass e-mails to the entire group. It was all too much for the poor e-mail server, which promptly gave up the ghost.

Endless love

An impassioned e-mail epistle became an Internet hit after it was forwarded by so many people that it eventually made the headlines. Joseph Dobbie had briefly met Kate Winsall at a barbecue and decided to woo her with an e-mail of Shakespearean proportions. Describing her smile as "the freshest of my special memories," he added that he was sure she would "be able to see sincerity where others would see cliché."

Of Ms. Winsall's smile, Dobbie enthused, "I will call on it when I am disheartened or low. I will hold it in my heart when I need inspiration. I will keep it with me for moments when I need to find a smile of my own."

Around 500 words later the outpouring ends on a high note: "If you are half as intelligent and aware as I believe you to be, I am sure that you will find what

I have written, in the very least, sweet. If I am twice as lucky as I would dare to hope, you will find this note charming and agree to contact me and arrange a date."

Alas, Kate played hard to get by forwarding the e-mail to her sister, who entitled it "How to ask a girl out (in a roundabout way)" and sent it to all her friends. The self-confessed "philosopher and poet" was bombarded with phone calls from around the globe.

Between you and me...

A lawyer working for pharmaceutical company Eli Lilly fell victim to a tool that was designed to make e-mail more efficient but which all too often causes disaster: address autocomplete. You can picture the scenario: You type in the first few letters of your intended recipient's name and up pops their full e-mail address— so handy, so convenient. Except when autocomplete gets it wrong.

In this case, the lawyer was representing Eli Lilly in confidential talks with the government about a billion-dollar fine and had intended to e-mail her co-counsel. But autocomplete had other ideas and instead inserted the e-mail address of a *New York Times* reporter who shared the same last name. The story made front-page news the very next day.

Come again?

And who can forget the now notorious "Claire Swire e-mail" of 2000, in which the London law-firm employee allegedly e-mailed Bradley Chait, another lawyer, about an intimate episode they'd enjoyed the previous night, during which she had obligingly performed a sex act upon him. Recalling the inevitable conclusion of their moment of passion, she wrote, "Yours was yum." Chait, no doubt delighted by this appraisal of his sexual prowess, forwarded the e-mail to his friends, who forwarded it to their friends, and so on. Within three days the e-mail had been read by an estimated 1 million people around the world.

Massive e-mail mess-ups

"I once e-mailed a new female client with details of a recently agreed deal, politely signing off, 'If you require further clarification, don't hesitate to contact me.' Or so I thought. I must have misspelled "clarification," prompting the hi-tech computer to insert its own guess. Ten minutes later I received a horrified response from the client in question: 'Matt, why on EARTH would I require further lubrication?'"

"A helpful recruitment person at my company sent an employee phone extension list to everyone at our company. But the spreadsheet had hidden columns that were easily unhidden to reveal everyone's pay, bonuses and stock options—including senior management's."

"Though I didn't know her well outside work, I always had a friendly relationship with the girl who worked at our reception desk. She knew everything that went on in the office and would often e-mail me tidbits of juicy gossip—who was sleeping with whom, who'd get outrageously drunk and phone in sick, etc. One day we had a new intern, whom I recognized immediately: He was the eighteen-year-old "toyboy" my twenty-five-year-old roommate had brought home from a party about a month previously and whom I'd overheard making strange, high-pitched noises in her bedroom. I knew the story would make my receptionist friend laugh, so I e-mailed her with all the details. About a half hour later I got a reply that made me want to curl up and die; it just said, 'That's my little brother.'"

The Office Holiday Party

"Work consists of whatever a body is obliged to do, and play consists of whatever a body is not obliged to do."

—*Mark Twain*

THERE'S only one thing that can make the heated house atmosphere of the office even more combustible than it already is: alcohol. And there's only one annual event at which the two are combined with such flagrant disregard for the consequences: the office holiday party.

Very few of us have ever remained sober long enough to work out how exactly these events unravel into such inevitable scenes of macabre debauchery. One minute everyone is chatting awkwardly and sipping warm drinks out of plastic cups, and the next the ambulances are arriving to peel the secretary off the ceiling and remove shards of glass from the chubby backside of the chief financial officer.

People who have never said more than "Good morning" to each other can find themselves playing strip football using someone's desk plant as a ball just a few short hours into that one special night. Meanwhile, rivals who have quietly plotted against each other all year let loose with their mutual loathing via big, screechy, hair-pulling fights: By the time "White Christmas" comes on, however, they're crying and clinging to each other, professing everlasting friendship.

The morning after is sickening in every way imaginable as fragmented memories of the previous night's chaos filter in with the kind of obscene hangover that can only be caused by complete immersion of the liver in pure vodka.

Modern mortification

In days of yore, the one consolation was that everyone else felt as bad as you did and you were all too drunk to remember any of it. But nowadays the comforting ethos of "What happens at the Christmas party *stays* at the Christmas party" has been ripped to shreds. The camera phone, now updated to include state-of-the-art video-recording equipment, has pulled ancient office traditions up by the roots. Thousands of compromising scenes have already been uploaded to YouTube, offering a terrifying insight into what we ourselves must look like every year.

In one such clip, a woman drunkenly lists her boss's many failings on camera, oblivious to the fact that he is standing right behind her looking seriously unimpressed. In another, a wildly intoxicated man throws up into his glass, pauses for a moment to give it a pensive stir, and then carries on drinking.

According to one survey, as many as 7 percent of office parties lead to an official warning or dismissal, with "improper sexual conduct" reported at an additional 4 percent.

Top 5 things guaranteed to happen at the office holiday party

There are some things that are bound to happen at some point during the course of the evening, whether you remember them the next day or not.

1. The mismatched coupling: This is probably more distressing to witness than to participate in. The most dramatic cases are when the office babe, who is so attractive that no sane person would ever risk making a move on her, gets caught under the mistletoe with the loner from accounts who looks like a warthog but knows a move or two on the dance floor.

2. The "boss is behind you" moment: This is a phenomenon that can usually be observed from about halfway through the office party, when our usual inhibitions have been beaten into submission by several hours of steady drinking and we're seeking to bond with our colleagues over shared hardships. It may be that you've told a little-known anecdote that highlights your boss's extreme stupidity, or perhaps done a brilliant impression of them, when you notice darting eye movements and frantic head-jerking from your formerly appreciative audience.

3. Solitary partner syndrome: There is no more inappropriate place for a spouse than the office holiday party. It's hard enough to integrate your beloved with your colleagues when the latter are sober; when they're all drunk and surviving on "office humor," it's simply torture. But someone always does it, and for some desperate portion of the evening, you will find yourself trapped in a corner with the shell-shocked husband of Maud from payroll, whose pastime is collecting photographs of electricity pylons. The only way out is to feign a sudden urge to use the bathroom, but escape comes at a price: You'll be haunted for the rest of the night by his lonely presence at the edge of the room while Maud dances provocatively on the desks.

4. Bossy behavior: For the first three or four hours of the holiday party, the boss usually retains an air of studied aloofness, either in a bid to seem dignified or because no one is willing to talk to him until they're three spreadsheets to the wind. But there is always that unforgettable window, after the whisky kicks in but before the sense of shame has a chance to, when the boss really joins the party. It usually coincides with some best-forgotten rock song being played at full volume; something about those repetitive riffs unleashes his inner rock god and suddenly he's away, the tie is off, the collar is open a good three buttons beyond decency, and he really lets it rip. Just make sure you have your cameras poised.

5. The holiday office love-in: No matter how much you've loathed them during the course of the year—and indeed during the first half of the holiday party—there comes a moment when you look around at the bleary-eyed faces of your colleagues and feel a sudden and inexplicable surge of love. In their wine-spattered outfits and crumpled party hats, their bad manners and disgusting habits seem rather sweet and endearing. Who, after all, are the people you spend all day with, who actually understand what it is you do, who know how you take your coffee?

Not the friends and relations you sandwich into the scant hours of evenings and weekends, but this team—this motley band of brothers doing the conga round the watercooler! You grab the nearest polyester-clad waist and hug it out.

Swapping Secret Santas

But the office holiday celebration unfortunately doesn't end at the party. No, it must take place instead on the last day in the office, when everyone is desperate to be somewhere else and no one wants

yet another piece of plastic junk to have to carry home on the train.

Why we persist with this dreadful faux "tradition," which was actually only invented in the 1980s and causes nothing but irritation and misery, is beyond explanation, but by the time we suggest the possibility of *not* doing one, some penny-pinching harridan in customer relations has already bought her item in the end-of-summer sale and won't be persuaded to cancel the ordeal.

There's usually a fairly low spending limit for these detestable gifts, so "joke" items have become a popular way to avoid looking for anything nice. But just because it's a joke doesn't mean it's any less awful. For instance, take a look at the list that follows, of the world's worst Secret Santa gifts, and be grateful you received the soap-on-a-rope.

* Ear-hair trimmers

* A bikini-line waxing kit

* Deodorant

* An enormous mesh bra

* A wig and a hairbrush

* A dog jacket

* A pile of well-thumbed
  magazines

* A child's car seat

* A voucher for office supplies

* A bag of caramel popcorn from
  the office kitchen

* A handmade certificate for
  membership to an online dating
  website

* Wineglasses clearly stolen
  from a budget airline

* Hairbrush with hair still wrapped around it

* A pair of purple tights with a tear in the crotch

* A protractor

* A set of inflatable boxing gloves

* A blow-up sheep

* A guide to the U.S. waterways

* A giant Toblerone so out of date that the chocolate had turned white

* A three-inch-tall clown made from blown Venetian glass

* A "vintage" edition of Scrabble that was missing six letters and had someone else's doodles all over the scorekeeping notepad

* A towel embroidered with the initials J.F.P.

You really shouldn't have

And it's no better when the giver of your gift knows it's you they're buying for. A list of genuine gifts given by bosses to their long-suffering assistants over the last few years makes for dispiriting reading:

- A signed and framed photograph of the boss looking manly behind his desk

- A light-up pair of reindeer horns that only light up on one side

- A set of itchy satin lingerie, three sizes too big and wrapped in a bag from Goodwill

- A book, along with a reminder that everyone will be expected to start work an hour earlier after New Year's

- A two-hour digitally remastered tape recording of the boss's annual sales conference speech in a "goodie bag" also containing rubber bands and paper clips

Bosses' Dastardly Ways

Boss: "Steve, I don't know how we'd
           get along without you."

Steve: "Thank you, sir."

Boss: "But we're going to try."

BOSSES must have been people once, but something happened to them, probably long before we were born, that turned them into cold-blooded machines. It's best not to spend too much time dwelling on how and why they came to lose their sense of compassion, their sense of family unity, their sense of moral justice, or indeed, their sense of style. Unless you plan on retraining as a psychotherapist and dedicating the rest of your life to talking them through their angst, you are never going to understand why they smile at you sweetly one day and look at you as though you've just burned their house down the next.

Instead, concentrate on observing their behavior in the style that wildlife-show presenters employ when observing the mating rituals of the Eritrean warthog.

Try to spot a pattern if you can, modifying your movements to avoid alarm and, most important, remaining at a safe distance. Even on those rare occasions when they seem accepting of your company, stay alert: They are highly volatile creatures and may turn on you if they feel their security is being threatened.

There are some that break the mold, of course, but poor communication skills, dishonesty, and a nasty habit of claiming responsibility for the hard work of their underlings has left a third of office workers pining for a new boss. Beware of what you wish for, though. Assess the behavior of your own tormentor against these real horror stories—your new boss could be even worse.

"My friend worked for an artist's agent who is famously nightmarish. She used to find him writhing on the floor having two-year-old-style tantrums, or smacking the desk with his fist if he didn't get his own way."

"I once had a new PR assistant working for me, and the s--- hit the fan with the account she was working on. I was busy and told her to explain to my boss the problem and the proposed course of action. The PR went over to his desk and had got as far as saying, 'We have a problem with a client,' when the boss put up his hands and shouted, 'Stop! Here we don't have problems; we only have solutions.'"

"My first boss refused to use a computer for any purpose whatsoever—this was 2003—and would dictate every single e-mail, letter, and memo at breakneck speed while the pungent fumes of his partially digested lunch wafted into my face. He'd send me on a constant stream of non-job-related errands (buying his child a birthday card, seeking out a replacement blade for his razor), from which I'd often return to find an empty water bottle on my desk with a Post-it note: 'Please fill.'"

"I had a boss who had an interesting way of getting someone to help him. He was head of a small film company and ruled the place like a little dictator— he'd regularly shout and swear at us, and new employees usually spent their first few weeks in tears. He was one of those men who deliberately couldn't do anything for himself—one of us even had to choose his tie for him—and when he was in his office with the door closed and wanted one of us to attend to him, he would bellow 'Service!' at the top of his voice."

"My first boss was a bit of a sleaze. He made no secret of the fact that he liked to employ nubile young women and would often make excuses for them to come and visit him in his office. One day I made the mistake of wearing a short skirt to work—not excessively short, probably just above the knee—but still, my legs were out. I got an e-mail asking me to go and help him with his filing and, when I got there, found that he'd arranged all his papers on the floor so I would have to keep bending down to pick them up."

The world's worst bosses

Even these bad bosses seem mild-mannered compared to some; tyrannical top dogs have been around since the Stone Ages. Here are some of the worst bosses in recent, and not so recent, history.

Al Capone

The notorious mobster was known as a ruthless boss and ruled his gang, the Chicago Outfit, like a dynastic emperor throughout the 1920s. He was brutal in the treatment of his enemies—he was responsible for the prearranged killing of seven men during the

St. Valentine's Day Massacre of 1929 and ordered the killing of dozens more of his rivals—but he was equally merciless with his own employees. He had police and Congressmen on his payroll, as well as an army of around a thousand gunmen. There were no appraisals or three-step warning systems in this particular outfit; anyone he thought might betray him was simply "bumped off."

Field Marshall Douglas Haig

There has been widespread academic debate as to the fairness of Field Marshall Haig's nickname, the "Butcher of the Somme," but whether or not he deserves to be vilified for his role in the dreadful number of losses sustained on the battlefields of France during the First World War, you certainly wouldn't have wanted to be working under him. His old-fashioned faith in the power of the cavalry and his blind determination to keep sending troops "over the top" into machine-gun fire they could never to survive gained him a reputation as an unfeeling and incompetent commander.

J. Edgar Hoover

The former FBI director was a tyrannical leader whose own disregard for the law when it came to amassing power at the expense of his underlings earns him a place among the world's worst bosses. Throughout his forty-eight years at the FBI, he used his privileged position to compile secret dossiers on prominent political figures in order to enhance his own status. He encouraged the use of illegal methods to obtain evidence, displayed open hostility toward African Americans, and launched a hate campaign against Martin Luther King, Jr.

There are also rumors that Hoover facilitated the Mafia's rise in power by refusing to investigate allegations against them, since they had allegedly obtained pictures of him in drag.

Jim Bakker

The TV evangelist and founder of the scarily successful Praise the Lord network set himself up as one of the world's most compassionate leaders, spreading the word of God and encouraging spiritual devotion, selflessness, and compassion for the poor. In 1987, however, it emerged that his so-called "non-profit" enterprise was somehow allowing him and his wife to live in a luxurious $600,000 Palm Springs mansion with a Rolls-Royce, four condominiums in California, and annual salaries of $200,000 each. He was eventually indicted for tax fraud, but further bad-boss behavior came to light when it was revealed that Bakker had paid off his former secretary to stay silent about their adulterous affair.

Nice man.

Ken Lay

The disgraced former head of Enron earned his position as one of the worst bosses of the new millennium when he repeatedly reassured employees that the company was financially secure despite knowing that it was in fact on its last legs. While publicly refuting claims that the company was going to fold, he was secretly selling off his own 918,000 shares of company stock. When Enron went bankrupt in December 2001, 20,000 of his employees lost their jobs, and many of them also lost their life savings, which were invested in the company. Merry Christmas, one and all.

Bernie Madoff

A former non-executive chairman of the NASDAQ stock exchange and CEO of his own securities company, Bernie Madoff was convicted of operating the largest investor fraud ever committed by an individual. He was estimated to have lost his investors a total of almost $65 billion by running a "Ponzi" scheme, whereby investors are paid out of their own money or with money from other investors, rather than from any real profit.

International fraud aside, Madoff's secretary revealed his more ordinary irritating-boss side, saying that he was a sexist, egomaniacal, short-tempered control freak who would try to slap her backside and who handled stress by making insulting comments to his staff. In 2009, he was sentenced to 150 years in jail for the fraud part of his bastardly behavior.

Sir Fred Goodwin

The former chief executive of the Royal Bank of Scotland was responsible for the large-scale expansion of the bank, which subsequently made losses of £24.1 billion (U.S. $39.8 billion), the biggest in U.K. corporate history. He was known for his lavish spending on fancy new head offices and use of a Falcon jet for corporate travel, and was listed as one of the 25 individuals at the heart of the world financial meltdown of 2008. He made an estimated £20 million (U.S. $33.1 million) from the bank, and then left, leaving the taxpayer to foot the bill for its rescue, insulting his thousands of newly pink-slipped former employees by arranging a payoff on top of a £16 million (U.S. $27 million) pension.

Getting your own back:
Acts of revenge

The one benefit of having a really bad boss is that there's no gray area in your mind, as to your opinion about them. If they have proved, through many years of mental torture and professional neglect, that they are rotten to the core, you can plot your revenge without so much as a moment's hesitation—and 6 in 10 of us who have been badly treated by a boss do eventually get revenge.

Just be absolutely sure that your boss can never find out that it was you; if you thought they made your life hell when you were pretending to like them, imagine how bad things could get if they knew the lengths you were willing to go to see them suffer. Take inspiration from these real tales of getting even:

One secretary filled the air vents in her boss's car with talcum powder before he was due to drive important clients to dinner. When he started the engine, the car was filled with a sweet-smelling but very messy white powder that got all over his suit, hair and face, and all over the guests he was so eager to impress.

A personal assistant who had spent years at the mercy of her mean-spirited boss let herself into his office while he was away and injected milk into his chair. She also bought a packet of coldcuts and spread it thinly under the carpet of his office. By the time he returned from his vacation, the smell of rancid meat and sour milk was so horrific that his office had to be steam-cleaned.

A junior secretary who had been badly treated by her boss the week before a big presentation hijacked his moment in the spotlight by swapping his carefully prepared notes for some completely irrelevant documents.

An angry marketing manager who had been told she couldn't attend an event that she had single-handedly organized got her revenge on her boss by resetting the security code on his briefcase. He had to run the whole event without being able to refer to the preparatory work she'd done, with no clue as to the answers to various questions fired at him.

A boss who always sent his assistant on personal errands and asked her to make him up to 10 cups of coffee a day in his freshly cleaned "special mug" got his payback when she found that the most efficient way to keep his precious mug sparkling was to put it in the toilet and flush.

A secretary whose philandering boss turned nasty after she rebuffed his sexual advances found a novel way to teach him a lesson. Her sister was heavily pregnant at the time, so the secretary asked her to do a pregnancy test, which obviously came out positive, and then mailed the test to her boss without any explanation. When the package arrived for him, she opened it, as was customary, and screamed in dramatic horror so that everyone turned to see what he'd been sent.

A junior account manager at a marketing firm was treated as an errand boy by his boss. He was expected to pick up his dry-cleaning, purchase flowers for his wife's birthday, and fetch several coffees from a smart Italian coffeeshop throughout the day. One day the usual waitress wasn't at the coffeeshop, and the one who dealt with the order made a regular coffee instead of the boss's usual decaf. The junior noticed that his boss seemed jittery all morning, so he continued buying him full-strength coffee all day. By 5:00 P.M. the boss was suffering palpitations and had to visit the office nurse.

The Office: Your Second Home

"Hard work never killed anybody, but why take a chance?"

—*Edgar Bergen*

G IVEN that we spend the majority of our waking hours at the office, it seems only fair that we should introduce a few home comforts. Decorative flourishes that personalize your little square of space can create a welcome oasis in the barren uniformity of the office wilderness.

Position your screen for privacy. If the office is to truly feel like your second home, you need to know that Derek in Payroll isn't leering over your shoulder every time you update your Facebook profile. If the open-plan layout makes privacy impossible, put a cushion behind your head or go for a Marge Simpson hairstyle that will shield your screen from view.

Create your own botanical garden. The Aspidistra Elatior is the perfect starting plant, since it can survive in most hostile environments (that is, offices) and has large paddlelike leaves that create a comforting canopy around you. Tending to your own plants can also be wonderfully therapeutic; give the leaves a gentle dusting next time you have a run-in with the photocopier and note how quickly your heart rate returns to normal.

Feng shui your office. Channel the ancient powers of the East to enhance your own positive energy while sending negative feng shui signals over to your rival across the room. Directing a draft toward them is the most surefire way to bring them bad luck, but if you can't persuade the air-conditioning man to dirty his hands by colluding with your scheming ways, simply arrange a small pile of clutter near their desk.

Invest in reversible wall art. Think back to your school days when your half-naked poster of Keanu

Reeves or Pamela Anderson had to be cunningly concealed on the inside cover of your ring binder. These very same techniques apply in adulthood. Simply stick Hugh Jackman, Bradd Pitt, or Rihanna on the back of your Fire Regulations printout and pin it up in such a way that the eye candy can be concealed with the subtlest flick, should the boss wander past.

Get all the modern conveniences. The surge in insurance claims for work-related ailments such as back pain, carpal tunnel syndrome, or eyestrain mean that there has never been a better time to present your boss with your office-furniture wish list. Maybe you'd like to experiment with sitting on a bouncy Swiss ball chair? Or perhaps your tired forearms would benefit from Robocop-style wrist rests that practically do your typing for you? It's all there for the taking.

Share your feelings. Create a communal "wall of love" and "wall of hate." Encouraging your colleagues to stick up pictures of anyone or anything who has created a spark or irritated them can lead to great conversation. But beware: One former office employee revealed that they had a wall of lust where they stuck pictures of their crushes. "Once a topless picture of Tony Blair playing tennis appeared overnight. No one ever owned up to it."

Discover your inner conceptual artist. Decorate your space with "found objects." Driftwood and white pebbles tend not to wash up on the carpet tiles of your average office, but there are plenty of readily available items that can be crafted into stylish urban alternatives. Paper-clip chains and Sticky Tack sculptures make wonderful contemporary design statements.

Cultivate a mold garden. If conventional plant life sounds too much like hard work, then strike out instead into the newly fashionable world of "grime gardening." Replace potted plants and seedlings with old mugs and half-eaten sandwiches. Given time and carefully maintained neglect, a miniature forest of life will soon spring up around you. Alexander Fleming discovered penicillin using similar methods.

Analyze your habits. Decorate your wall with a map of your hometown and stick a yellow pin everywhere you've had a drink. Then stick a blue pin everywhere you've done something you regret. When you get bored of staring at your own failings, add someone else's. One publishing assistant made a Map of Literary Failure by sticking pins in the hometowns of people who'd sent in awful manuscripts. Apparently, there was a hotspot in a small town just outside Birmingham, Kentucky.

Lunch Break Adventures

"I couldn't really see the point of having lunch unless it started at one and ended a week later in Monte Carlo."

—*Arthur Smith, musician*

ALTHOUGH the average employee is entitled to a total of 240 lunch hours each year, a ridiculous 75 percent of us don't take them, opting instead to stare blank-eyed at our computer screens while speedily stuffing over-refrigerated sandwiches into our mouths and scattering crumbs into the nooks and crannies of our keyboards.

There may be no escaping the day-in, day-out drudgery of the 9 to 5, but there *is* a way of reclaiming this little fragment of time in the middle of every workday. The vast untapped reserve of daylight hours that is rightfully yours adds up to 10 full days of glorious free time per year, so get out there and make the most of it.

Shed 10 years

For decades, scientists have been researching away in their laboratories just so that you can step out and have your cheeks buffed up on your lunch break. There are, at this very moment, universities full of tomorrow's plastic surgeons performing the same puncture-syringe-swab movement so that procedures that used to require an overnight stay and a week of recovery can be done in less time than it takes to run to McDonald's and back. Collagen injections, Botox, lip plumping, eyebrow lifting, spider-vein removal, and tooth whitening can all be slotted into a lunchtime schedule. With just one short session a month, you could have a whole new face by the end of the year.

Go on a date

This is a great one for distracting yourself from the tedium of work. Not only does it make your lunch break itself more interesting, but it makes the morning fly by in nervous anticipation. You can also spend most of the afternoon dissecting the pros and cons of your date's personality and deciding whether or not you want to arrange a second rendezvous. Either sign up for an organized lunchtime dating event—several speed-dating events for busy professionals now take place on the lunch hour—or get your friends to set you up on a blind date. Having to get back to the office is the perfect excuse to get you out of lingering over coffee if it turns out not to be a match made in heaven.

Mix yourself a cocktail

Sometimes the only way to calm your nerves after a morning from hell is the old-fashioned way: by drinking a good stiff cocktail. Throwing a few back on your lunch hour at a local restaurant is obviously the safest and most socially acceptable way to lift your spirits, but unfortunately, it's usually the days when you don't have time to get out and lunch ends up being an egg-salad sandwich al fresco that the urge to hit the bottle strikes hardest.

What's required in these circumstances is subterfuge. There are two highly effective methods by which to drink in the office without getting caught. One is a cocktail known as Job's on the Rocks.

4 ounces of strong cold medicine
1 packet of sugar or spoonful of honey
1 miniature bottle of vodka (alternative recipes include
brandy for traditionalists, or cassis if you prefer a
blackcurrant mixer)
1 squeeze of fresh lemon

The beauty of this method is twofold. First, the lemony fumes will mask the incriminating scent of booze; second, if the intoxicating effects begin to show themselves, you can pass them off as symptoms of your terrible cold. Short-term memory loss, drowsiness, flushed cheeks, and a red nose can all be attributed to feverish delirium and too much nose blowing.

And if anyone does catch you tippling, you can claim it's simply a medicinal hot toddy like Grandma used to make.

For a more celebratory occasion, a green-tinted San Pellegrino plastic bottle is the perfect disguise for some bubbly. Simply pour away the contents and replace with the proper fizz.

The bubble ratio is strikingly similar, and the colored plastic hides the color of your illicit aperitif. The one snag is the smell: a 250-ml serving of champagne can cause even the hardiest office drinker to tilt slightly toward whomever they may be talking to. Should that person be rude enough to suggest there is a whiff of debauchery about you, you need to be prepared with the right response: Lean forward an inch, sniff gently, and say, "Now that you mention it, I can smell alcohol. Or is it antiseptic?"

Have a massage

Sixty hours a week hunched over a keyboard can do terrible things to your posture, not to mention the risk of repetitive strain injury posed by the thousands of tiny muscle movements required to move your mouse, so use your lunch break to counteract the havoc wreaked on your body from office life. Many massages last a lunch hour–friendly 45 minutes; if you're a few minutes late back to your desk, your newfound Zen-like aura of calm will stop you from worrying. Take your pick of massage techniques, from the bone-cracking to the brain-soothing— whatever you go for will have you floating back to the office with your head full of sunbeams—though possibly also with your hair full of geranium oil.

Expand your mind

Have you ever blamed the lack of hours in the day for your reluctance to take a class? Well, you have no excuse. The average language class lasts between 40 and 50 minutes, leaving you plenty of time to get there and back at lunchtime while practicing your vocab on the bus. And if language lessons bring back too many painful memories of that awful foreign exchange you were forced to do at age 14, find something else to fill your head. Many art galleries and museums offer lunchtime talks and lectures (which make one sound terribly cultured and interesting at dinner parties, darling), while distance-learning courses that require just an hour's work a day can be slotted in wherever you take your lunch break.

Have your fortune told

"Cross my palm with silver and look to the skies. Ahh, yes, I see a lover with come-to-bed eyes." Well, that's usually how it goes, isn't it? Anyway, the future is a hell of a lot more interesting than most days at the office, and with most astrology readings taking less than half an hour, it's the perfect contrast to the *Groundhog Day* sameness of eating "Pasta Excursion" in the staff cafeteria. And don't worry: You don't have to flag down a passing circus to get your palm read these days. There are mystics and mind readers all over the place— some have even set up stalls in department stores and see clients on a first-come, first-served basis. Perfect for a spontaneous spurt of lunch-hour excitement (depending on what your future holds, of course).

Do something good

Volunteering isn't just about helping old people—although they are generally very appreciative of anyone who is willing to take on the task. Since the start of the century, volunteer work has surged in popularity. Some people do it to feel they're giving something back to society; some say it's the most rewarding part of their lives; others do it just to get something on their résumé that will help them escape from their present job.

Whatever your motivation, consider the possibility of offering up your lunch hour once in a while. Employers usually look kindly on this because it makes them look socially conscientious, and you might get a lot out of it, too. Volunteer organizations that offer placement in a range of different charities are a good place to start, unless your office happens to be down the road from an old folk's home.

Dance the hour away

Sometimes what is lacking in the course of a day at the office is a little bit of spice. Our habits are so ingrained and our interactions so strictly defined by office etiquette that unless we're playing with fire and considering an office fling, there's no chance for any kind of real human interaction. Which is why finding a dance class—like salsa or the lindy or even the tango—to fill your lunch break is such an appealing prospect.

For that precious window in your day, you can change out of your work clothes, let down your hair, and work up a sweat with another human being. Or, if your local daytime classes are filled with doddering retirees and the long-term unemployed, pick a style of dance that doesn't require close physical contact, like flamenco or street dance.

Take time to meditate

Ommmmmmmmmmmm...Come on, try it. Meditation has long been known by monks, mullahs, and yogis to produce a sense of rested, emotional stability and complete clarity of mind. But now their whimsical musings have been backed up by actual science. Brain scans carried out on experienced practitioners in the act of meditation show that the process stimulates the left prefrontal cortex, the part of your brain that generates feelings of contentment and happiness.

Meditation classes are best way to master the technique, but for a lunchtime quickie, listening to a downloaded guide on your iPod in any quiet spot will reap the same rewards.

After a morning spent listening to a presentation on "how to achieve core functionality within the corporate framework," a few happy brainwaves are probably just what you need.

Start a lunchtime book group

This is not just an excuse to have a nice long lunch over a few bottles of wine—although that is, of course, the added bonus of any literary pursuit—it's a chance to keep your brain engaged and make you look intellectual on the train to work. A book club is also the perfect environment for justified chatting. If you ran off on your lunch break saying that you were going to socialize at the local bar, you might raise a few eyebrows; if you saunter out with a hefty-looking tome under one arm, you morph into someone bright and articulate with a thrilling range of extracurricular activities that you somehow manage to squeeze in around work. And when you're not off to your book club, you can spend your lunch hour reading the next book.

Research your family tree

You never know, you might discover that you're the only surviving relative of a recently deceased earl or dictator somewhere in the world and that the executors of his will have been frantically searching for someone to claim his vast fortune. Or maybe you'll just find out that your grandmother made her living selling stolen goods and had an affair with a traveling salesman. Either way, it's good to remind yourself that the people you spend every waking moment with in the office are not, in fact, your family.

There is, of course, a wealth of information to help you trace your ancestors online, so you can do some research while pretending to look up sales figures or whatever it is you're paid to do. Use your free hour to get out and about; local municipal offices, newspaper archives, and libraries are good places to start.

The Sickie

"I still need more healthy rest in order to work at my best. My health is the main capital I have and I want to administer it intelligently."

—*Ernest Hemingway*

YOU'RE sitting at your desk one gray, drizzly Tuesday afternoon, drinking your vending-machine mochaccino and idly scrolling through the budget-DVD section on eBay, when suddenly it hits you: You don't have to be here. There is a whole world of dreadful illnesses you can fabricate in order to take a day off.

You could ask for a day's vacation, of course, but that takes all the fun out of deceiving your boss. And anyway, curling up on the sofa all morning and then having a quick stroll around the shops while there are no crowds isn't a vacation as such; it's recuperation—crucial rehabilitation, in fact.

Because now that you really come to think about it, you *are* sick. Sick of the tinted windows that filter out the sunlight, and the fluorescent lighting that makes everyone look jaundiced. Sick of the flavorless cafeteria sandwiches, the petty one-upmanship, and the tedious tit-for-tat gossip that poses as office politics. And sick, most of all, of the constant whir of machine-generated white noise that fills your head, slowly eradicating your capacity for independent thought and sautéing your brain cells until you emerge 10 years later as a bewildered and deeply neurotic departmental manager.

The really sick thing, if you think about it, would be *not* to take the sick leave. But we must tread carefully: Employers are on to us. A recent report found that workers took an average of 6.7 days' off for illness, 1 in 10 of which was thought to be of the less-than-genuine variety. These illegitimate "sickies" cost national economies billions each year, with call centers and communications companies reporting the worst rates of absenteeism.

The preparations

If you take the brave step of going home sick from work, you will need to be confident in both your acting skills and your factual information. Follow these steps in the runup to your announcement, or use them to pave the way for The Phone Call (see page 109) the next day.

1. Spread the word that there is illness in the air at least one day before you want to take your sick day. Tell colleagues that your partner/sister/cat has come

down with something awful, and throw in a few carefully researched symptoms, emphasizing how relieved you are that you haven't succumbed.

2. On the day itself, buy an extra sandwich at lunchtime and wolf down the first where no one can see you. Leave the decoy sandwich unopened on your desk. If anyone asks why you haven't had your lunch yet, shrug weakly and say you just don't feel hungry.

3. Keep your coat on at your desk no matter how warm the recycled air in your office becomes, rub your hands together in the manner of a Dickensian street urchin, and comment on how cold it feels.

4. If your complexion is revealingly ruddy and radiates health, there is a range of cosmetics that can help you effect that ghostly pallor without looking as if you're dressed for Halloween. Products designed for people prone to facial redness are particularly effective, ontaining a green tint that tones down any hint of pinkness.

5. In a loud but nontheatrical voice, telephone a friend who has been briefed on your scheme and pretend to cancel an arrangement that evening.

Tell them you're not feeling well and you need to rest because you've got a big day in the office tomorrow.

The Phone Call

The Phone Call itself is the only distasteful task you will have to perform all day. Execute it well and you're home free; mess up your lines and your much-needed day off will be marred by a niggling feeling that they're on to you. Use these tips to get it right.

Research your condition. Know what you've got and how it's making you feel. A vague description will sound wishy-washy and may arouse suspicion, so think of your alibi and stick to it.

Don't give too many details at once. You need to save some for your return to work, so one well-placed factoid will suffice.

Try to speak to an assistant or other person whose job will only be to pass on your message rather than to judge it for authenticity. This may mean making your call after the office opens but just before your boss arrives.

Make the call within one minute of your alarm going off and before you've spoken to anyone else, which should allow for maximum croakiness.

Try lying on your bed with your head hanging off the edge while placing the call—your voice will sound strangely congested.

Don't hesitate. If you say anything that suggests you're "not sure" if you can make it in or think you "might not be up to it," you'll look pathetic and wheedling. It's much better to err on the side of exaggeration. Say instead that you struggled out of bed and left the house but reluctantly had to turn back after a near-fainting incident in front of an oncoming taxi.

Play the contagious card. If your workplace is one of the many that subscribe to the "sickness is for wimps" business model, stick to faking uncomfortable or embarrassing illnesses that are highly contagious. Sometimes the threat of dhobie's itch (a catching fungal infection of the groin) is the only thing that will do.

Sickie symptoms made simple

Use this handy guide to planning your period of absence, but remember: Less is more. Give one or two symptoms and save the full description for your return to work.

One day off

Migraine: The main symptom is an intense headache, but other, less-well-known effects of a migraine may add authenticity. These include visual disturbances, such as flashing lights or blind spots, stiffness or tingling in your neck or shoulders, nausea, and increased sensitivity to light, sound, and smells.

Food poisoning (Campylobacter): This is a surefire winner, since the symptoms are so disgusting that even the most hard-to-fool boss would rather grant you your sick day than hear all the gory details. Explain that you are vomiting and have urgent diarrhea—the use of the word "urgent" in this context usually winds up the conversation fairly quickly.

Toothache: This is an oft-overlooked ailment in the sickie-options folder, which can make it a good one if your colleagues have used up all the usual suspects. An abscess lodged beneath a back tooth causes searing pain, a foul taste in the mouth, and can even result in a fever, with shivers, hot flushes, and bouts of delirium.

Two days off

Ear infection: If you've left it too late to act as if you're coming down with something nasty and need something with a sudden onset, an ear infection might be just the ticket. They often begin with a dull ache that you would think nothing of before suddenly turning nasty. An ear infection is characterized by a sharp pain deep in the ear, fever, and dulled hearing.

Stomach bug: Unlike food poisoning, a viral stomach bug can take longer to run its course and has the added advantage of leaving you feeling weak and dehydrated even once the worst effects—vomiting, diarrhea, headaches, and chills—have abated.

Laryngitis: This is an inflammation of the larynx and affects the vocal chords, so if you've perfected your croaky voice but want to keep it simple, this is a good contender. It usually clears up within a week, but you'll need to keep up the frog-in-throat act for a couple of days after your return to work.

Three to five days off

Strep throat: A more convincing-sounding version of tonsillitis, strep throat is caused by a bacterial infection that causes a painful throat with white patches on the tonsils and fever. It usually lasts about four days, and a trip to the doctor will be necessary for verification. (If you have no qualms, the treatment, if required, is penicillin.)

Flu: It can be difficult to get people to believe that you have the flu even when you really have it, since it can differ from the common cold only in the severity of its symptoms, but it's a good one for a three- to five-day break if you think you can pull if off. Emphasize the hot and cold flushes, aching joints, and high fever.

Conjunctivitis: Viral conjunctivitis is a contagious infection of the transparent surface membrane that covers the eye. It causes redness and stinging, and a yellowy crust often

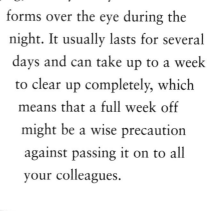

forms over the eye during the night. It usually lasts for several days and can take up to a week to clear up completely, which means that a full week off might be a wise precaution against passing it on to all your colleagues.

The Sickie Rules

1. Do not go *anywhere* where your colleagues are likely to see you looking healthy. Having a picnic in the park opposite your office may seem like the perfect way to relish the fact that you're not in it, but it won't go down well with the colleagues to whom you've been bare-facedly lying.

2. If you do venture out, keep a paper bag from your local pharmacy in your pocket at all times. If you see an oncoming coworker, whip out the bag and clutch it to you pathetically in case the need to justify your jaunt should arise.

3. Beware of leaving a telltale electronic trail; excessively animated tweeting or posting photos of your day off are sickie suicide. Remember, Big Brother is watching you, so keep as low a (Facebook) profile as possible.

4. Never attempt to pull a free sick day at a time of national sickie-pulling: sports finals, the first heat wave of summer, the day after a public holiday, etc. Your attendance at work on such occasions counts for double that of a normal day and will earn you brownie points that you can then freely spend on a day of your own choosing.

5. If you plan to play hooky on your birthday, take some time to come to terms with the fact that this means you must *not* mention your birthday at work; otherwise, your fake illness will be exposed in seconds. This is a challenging undertaking. It will mean no cake, no after-work drinks, no proudly howing off your presents. On the plus side, you obviously get to eat cake and drink beer with your real friends in the comfort of your own home.

6. Take five minutes at the start of your day off to check what's on TV at 3:00 P.M. The best corroboration of your bed-bound state is if you can say with conviction that you tried to watch TV but *Murder, She Wrote* was just too taxing.

10 great excuses for time off work

1. Your cat has been run over and requires immediate life-saving surgery. Make sure you sound shaken and tearful when you make the call.

2. Your partner/roommate has locked you in and gone on a business trip to Dubai. The great thing about this one is that you're at the mercy of the imaginary locksmith, whose timing is often atrocious with him being so in demand these days.

3. Your house has been broken into. The police will usually need to make several visits, and statement-giving can last all day.

4. There's been an anthrax scare at the post office down the road, and you've been told by police to stay indoors. This one would have sounded ridiculous 10 years ago, but sadly we've lived with terrorist alerts for so long now that incidents such as these are more common than a burst water pipe.

5. You've been asked to be a witness in court. This is both feasible and unusual, which makes for a winning combination. It's also fairly bulletproof, since anyone telephoning the courts to check up on your story could put themselves under suspicion of trying to intimidate a witness.

6. You've dropped your phone down a drain

while standing at the bus stop. This implies that you were up and dressed *and* on your way to work when you were waylaid by the hand of fate, which is always impressive.

7. You have become the victim of identity theft

and can't leave the house in case the new "you" breaks in and establishes squatter's rights. This needs at least one day off for sorting out the logistics and could require a longer period of compassionate leave, given the emotional and psychological distress caused by such an attack on your fundamental sense of self.

8. You were hypnotized by an amateur at a live

show over the weekend, and hearing "My Heart Will Go On" by Celine Dion on the radio has returned you to your trance. You'll earn brownie points for having the foresight to call work despite believing yourself to be a walrus called Rocky.

9. You've had a call from a retirement home

across the country saying that one of its residents is claiming you as his secret grandchild. You have to drive there immediately to help talk him down from the tree he's currently camping out in. When you return to work, your boss will surely condone your act of kindness.

10. You've been given an unfair parking ticket

and are staging a sit-in protest at the police station. This is an easy one, because most of us can convincingly enact the anger we feel against unjust fines. Just make sure you don't give the details of where your car was parked, so that you avoid the possibility of local press and colleagues coming to cheer you on.

5 dreadful excuses for time off work

1. **Going to the dentist.** This is well-known code for "I have a job interview."

2. **Hideous delays on your bus/train route.** This is far too checkable in these technological times, and you face the awful possibility that a little-known colleague takes the same route.

3. **Someone died.** The death will need to be pretty traumatic for it to warrant a day off work, which will mean keeping tabs on who in your immediate family is supposedly dead or alive for the rest of your employment.

4. **I thought it was Saturday.** Seriously?

5. **Waiting for a plumber.** See "Going to the dentist," above.

Sleeping on the Job

Boss: "Helen, you really should have been here at 9:00 A.M."
Helen: "Why, what happened?"

THE clock on the wall is ticking gently, the lines of the scintillating report you're preparing seem to bend and blur, and the effects of last night's late-night vodka session are tugging your eyelids downward. You need sleep—just a little cat nap that would shake you out of your lethargy and refresh you for the challenging afternoon's brainstorming that lies ahead. It's not so much to ask for; in Japan there are Tatami rooms in many workplaces, where employees can have a quick snooze on a comfy wooden mat, so why shouldn't we use a bit of our break to snatch some precious shuteye if that's what our bodies are telling us they need?

Sadly, Western employment practices are stuck in the past, and bosses seem fixated with the idea that when we're at work, we should be awake the entire time.

Their shortsightedness forces us underground, employing shadowy methods to get our 40 winks.

The following top-secret methods have been tried and tested by some of the world's greatest slackers. Some are riskier than others, but as long as you cover your tracks and exercise due caution, you could soon be incorporating a Mediterranean-style siesta into your hectic daily schedule.

The faux faint

If you really need a substantial slumber, you have to be prepared to be caught in the act, so you'll need to put measures in place to back up your excuse. The best defense is to pretend you weren't asleep at all, but had, in fact, fainted away in the manner of a delicate Victorian waif.

Props are all-important here: an almost-full cup of water placed just out of reach to avoid spillages while you snooze, a wholesome-looking glucose bar with one bite taken out of it, and a small bottle of eucalyptus oil—the modern version of smelling salts—will set the scene perfectly. When your boss smugly prods you in the shoulder and demands to know why you're dribbling all over your keyboard, just rub your eyes woozily and sniff at the oil while murmuring softly that you must have fainted again.

The sleeping peacock

The most technically demanding of all the options, this is a high-risk strategy that has high rewards for those who master it. The method takes inspiration from the markings of peacocks and butterflies that confuse predators into believing that they have many eyes that are always open and on the lookout for danger.

First scan in a close-up photo of your own head and blow it up so it's life-size. Then load your printer with a sheet of address labels and print your full-size photo. Carefully cut out the eyes and stick them to your eyelids. Then open a manual on your desk or rest a printed document on your keyboard, nod your head, close your eyes, and sail away to Dreamland.

The lazy bathroom break

This works especially well for the hangover nap, since it combines a certain degree of privacy with direct access to the toilet, should you be overcome by a sudden wave of nausea.

Choose the cubicle that's the farthest from the door to minimize disruptions, put the seat down, and sit on it with your spine right back against the wall. Then place your hands on your knees with your palms side by side and facing upward and slowly fold your upper body over until your forehead is resting on your open palms. Curl your fingers up to cup the crown of your head and relax. In a sleep-deprived state you can sleep pretty much anywhere and still be comfortable. Just make sure you check the mirror before you venture back into the office—too long a sleep can leave telltale palm prints on your forehead.

The supply closet snore-fest

If you're a snorer, the risks of sleeping on the job are even greater than for your less-congested colleagues. In fact, in years of testing all the best-known methods, one nasally afflicted office dozer found that the only way to avoid detection was to find a small, secure room separate from the main office to settle down. This also has the significant advantage of providing the only fully horizontal sleeping surface available in the office environment.

His research revealed that his own body, aided by the dead weight of sleep, made the perfect barricade when wedged against the door of the office supply closet. Colleagues in search of Post-it notes and paper simply assumed the closet was locked, and he found he could sleep there quite soundly for a good 20 minutes before suspicions were aroused, at which point he could justifiably claim he'd become bewildered by the overwhelming range of paperclips and thus collapsed in a cold sweat.

The nightwatchman

For this method to be remotely workable, you need a co-conspirator you can trust completely. If there's any doubt in your mind that your chosen colleague might fail you, intentionally or otherwise, you don't stand a chance of nodding off. Get the right wingman, however, and this is one of the most satisfying office sleeping systems out there. You simply take turns to sleep while the other scans the room for signs of danger.

What makes this mutually beneficial method so good is that you can really let yourself go. Roll up your coat to make a good pillow, place a lock of hair or piece of blotting paper over your eyes as a sleeping mask, and really nestle in. If anyone important looms on the horizon, your nightwatchman sounds the alarm and you're safe.

The jailer's nod

This one is based on suggestions by sleep experts that a short power nap can be just as effective at providing a short-term energy boost as a longer sleep. It involves allowing yourself to experience stages one and two of your natural sleep pattern, but waking before you get into a deeper, REM sleep.

If the theory sounds scientific, the method couldn't be less so. Just sit in your chair with your arms on the armrests and hold your house keys in one hand. Allow yourself to drift off. When your muscles begin to relax at the end of stage two, you'll drop the keys and startle yourself into consciousness again. Because the whole process takes only 20 minutes and you never slip into a deep sleep, you're unlikely to get caught.

Circular Snooze

There are times when falling asleep on your keyboard simply isn't restful enough: I'm talking extreme hangovers and/or sleepless nights. In these situations you need more than a mere handful of stolen moments in the supply closet. What you need is sleep—dream-inducing, limb-relaxing, drool-producing sleep—and the only place you're going to get that is outside the confines of your office.

But where can you fall into such a blissful trance without rousing the suspicions of passersby? Look no further than your local public transportion system. Simply choose a bus or train route that travels back and forth over a short distance and set your phone's alarm for one hour later. It's amazing how quickly the sweaty, early-morning mess of irate commuters can give way to a sleepy lunchtime calm. You'll have your pick of the moderately comfortable seats and be lulled to sleep by the gentle rocking of the vehicle.

Sightseeing bus tours are particularly useful since they tend to do a huge loop in about an hour, delivering you back to wherever you started.

What to say if the boss *does* catch you catnapping

"Wow! That course you sent me on was so right: I feel full of inspiration after that power nap."

"Oh, hi. I was just meditating on the mission statement."

"They told me at the blood bank that I might feel sleepy."

"I was actually just testing a new neck exercise my physio has prescribed for my work-related back injury."

"My client said that workplace fatigue was a problem for her team—I was just trying to get into their mindset."

"All my best ideas come to me in dreams."

"I was just taking advice from my Native American spirit guide—he's always so good at identifying the golden thread."

"...in the name of the Father, the Son, and the Holy Spirit, Amen."

The World Wide Web

"Anyone can do any amount of work provided it isn't the work he is supposed to be doing at the moment."

—*Robert Benchley*

WHAT the heck did people do all day in the office before the arrival of the Internet? Really, isn't constant access to the rest of the world the one thing that actually persuades us to keep going back to the godforsaken office day in and day out? Have you ever had to sit for even half an hour without access to the Internet at work? Even as the IT nerd is rummaging with your cables, you can feel the tips of your fingers itching to get back on there. It's our lifeline, our bread and butter, our best friend, and boy, do we make the most of it.

Accessing the World Wide Web for all its myriad uses has got to be the best-ever way to waste valuable company time. The options are endless! Twenty-five percent of us happily download music at work,

14 percent play Web-based computer games, and a naughty 7 percent admit to downloading pornography in the office.

But keeping track of our friends and managing our social lives is the biggest user of our Web time. Younger workers are the most likely to use their employer's technology for personal reasons, and nearly three quarters regularly check personal e-mail accounts during office hours. Despite desperate attempts by frustrated employers to curb our personal use of the Internet while we're on their time, monitoring, legal warnings, and heavy-handed company policies have done nothing to dampen our enthusiasm, especially now that social networking has become such a central part of daily life.

Undercover surfing

Quite frankly, spending between 8 and 12 hours a day looking at a computer screen without checking personal e-mails, snooping at other people's photos, and bidding on eBay should classify as torture.

Unfortunately, it is in fact what most employers call "doing a day's work," so pursuing your personal interests on the Internet has to be done secretly. Here's how:

Create a domino effect

This works great if you're lucky enough to share your office with like-minded colleagues. There's usually at least one person with a good vantage point from which to see the boss approaching. When you see that person's Facebook profile vanish from their screen, you in turn hit the X on whichever Web page you happen to be browsing, thus passing the warning signal on to the colleague behind you. It's like smoke signals but without the fire risks.

Alternate tasks

Always keep a work-related document open on your desktop, with your little finger hovering over the "ALT" key. Pressing "ALT" and "TAB" will instantly switch from one screen to another, avoiding that giveaway scrabble for the mouse.

Test the waters

Be aware of the layout of your office. Do a dummy walk from the boss's office past your own desk and work out how much they can see and how best to time your screen switches.

Stop the glare

If your screen can be seen constantly by a senior colleague or office rival, arrange for a workspace assessment with your occupational health department and complain about the glare on your screen. This will allow you to move the screen or even shield it with a well-placed plant without arousing anyone's suspicions.

Stay terribly busy

Keep a notebook open on your desk with a to-do list of the day's work-related activities. Tick off tasks 1 and 2 and make number 3 "Get figures from Internet" or something similar that vaguely fits in with your remit. Then if anyone catches you surfing, you can just say you were led there by a rogue Web link. It's amazing how similar "Tangiers" and "Tangents" are when you type them into a search engine.

Minimize, minimize

Open several work-related documents and reduce each one in size so that you've got three or four open at once. Now open another for your personal use and keep it very small. You only need a tiny window into your own world to feel you have escaped the drudgery of the office.

Making
Personal Calls

Parkinson's Law: Work expands so as to fill
the time available for its completion.

O NE of the really annoying things about office life
is that it fills such a huge and useful chunk of the
day. Before 9:00 A.M., most of us are fit only for
conversations that comply with hangover and sleep-
deprivation regulations, such as whether we want
Crunchy Nut Cornflakes or peanut butter on toast for
breakfast and how much sugar we take in our coffee.
It would be both cruel and impractical to expect people
to make personal calls first thing in the morning.

The other end of the working day is just as tricky.
After the 9 or 10 hours we are compelled to spend
providing a running commentary on every workplace
decision we make, the idea of putting the vocal chords
to any other use than ordering the night's first gin and
tonic seems criminally inhumane.

So when are we supposed to fit in the conversations
that are necessary in order to keep up with our

personal lives? In the office, of course. There are three primary techniques utilized by experienced practitioners.

The Hoarse Whisperer

This is best for the timid of heart and has the advantage of allowing calls to be made at any time of day, with relatively low risk of detection. It is especially beneficial for a phone call that comes in at an awkward moment, like when your boss comes by for an update on your progress.

The idea is simply to effect a sore throat and speak in a very low voice, which you must allow to occasionally crack whenever you're required to say anything that might otherwise give the game away.

Good for: Making appointments with your doctor, dentist, or hairdresser, all of whom are so used to hearing people whine on at them in pathetically put-upon tones that they have begun to believe that that's just how most people speak. It may also help you get an earlier appointment.

Bad for: Making complaints to customer-service departments. Trying to sound threatening is a challenge when it's done in a whisper. The chances are high that whomever you're speaking to will take you for a spineless, flu-riddled weakling and brush you off by telling you that they "see where you're coming from but unfortunately can't change company policy."

The Secret Agent

Friendly discussions seem to be allowed as long as they're with colleagues or work associates in other organizations, so many serial personal-callers use this to their advantage.

For the method to work successfully, you need to mention your place of employment as if you're on friendly but businesslike terms with whomever you're speaking to. It also helps to ask for someone official-sounding by name. Your opening gambit might go along the lines of: "Hello, this is Katie from Orson Turnbull. Could I speak to Jeff in your PR department, please?" Anyone listening out for gossip will immediately swivel off elsewhere, leaving you to chat in peace.

Good for: Making weekend plans with friends who are sympathetic to the restrictions of the office environment. They will probably be using a similar technique at their end of the conversation, and over time you can establish complex fake work relationships.

Bad for: Dutiful calls to elderly relatives. Old Uncle Norman probably already thinks he's Napoleon, so it would be wrong to confuse him any more by addressing him as if he were Simon in Accounting.

The Foghorn

This is strictly for the brave of heart, because it will only work if everyone around you is too intimidated by your audacious disregard for office etiquette to complain. The idea is simply to go ahead and make your personal calls as if it were your God-given right. Go ahead—call your lover or your divorce lawyer!

Recent surveys have found that, since most of us work ridiculously long and unsociable hours, employers who allow us to make the occasional personal calls from our desks can expect greater staff loyalty, which in turn will lead us to work even longer hours.

Win-win (kind of).

Good for: Booking meals at restaurants. No one has to know it's only Pizza Hut.

Bad for: Consultations with any of your "ologists." The fact that you're having a bit of a problem with your bowels may be of interest to whomever you're paying to monitor them, but no one else wants to know.

Wasting Company Time

"Time is nature's way of keeping everything from happening at once."

—*Woody Allen*

PICTURE the scene: Thursday afternoon, 3:05 P.M. The clock is moving so slowly that you start to wonder whether some glitch in the space-time continuum has actually caused the world to come to a standstill—wasn't it 3:00 P.M. half an hour ago?—and yet the people around you seem to still be busying themselves with various work-related tasks.

Rumor has it that scientists are on the verge of proving that the hour between 3:00 P.M. and 4:00 P.M. is indeed four times longer than every other hour of the day, but that will come as little comfort to the millions of disillusioned office employees who traditionally spend this "hour" staring at the wall, too unmotivated even to chew their fingernails.

So what is there to do when you literally have nothing to do? Take heart: There are hundreds of

largely pointless but gratifyingly time-wasting activities in which you can indulge. The following list should provide you with at least a week's worth of futile fun.

- Collecting jokes and other humorous material from the Internet

- Forwarding jokes and other humorous material to your friends

- Faxing jokes and other humorous material to your parents

- Photocopying and then posting jokes and other humorous material to your grandmother

- Trying to sound knowledgeable while having no idea what you're talking about

- Thinking about what to have for lunch

- Waiting for the end of the day

- Composing a vicious verbal attack on a colleague

- Delivering a vicious verbal attack on a colleague

Regretting a vicious verbal attack on a colleague

Covering for the incompetence of a friend or colleague

Trying to remedy your bad-hair day

Trying to explain something to a colleague who is distracted by her own bad-hair day

Buying a snack

Eating a snack

Washing your hands and face to remove all evidence that there was any kind of snack in your vicinity

Fabricating expense claims

Inventing timesheet entries

Scratching yourself

Training yourself to sleep with your eyes open

Coming across your paystub and feeling shocked when reminded of how little you actually earn

Venting about a colleague

Venting about your boss

Venting about your boss's boss

Venting about family problems to a colleague who will hopefully never meet your relatives

Miscellaneous unproductive venting

Searching for a new job

Suffering from some sort of malaise

Preparing medication

Taking medication

Making an elaborate lunch

Taking it easy while digesting food

Using company resources for personal profit

Stealing office supplies—can be time-consuming because it has to be done in pocket-size portions

Chatting to your sister in Australia

Gossiping

Planning a party

Pretending to work while the boss is watching

Pretending to enjoy your job

Pretending to like your colleagues

Pretending to like important people while secretly thinking of ways to publicly humiliate them

Miscellaneous unproductive fantasizing

Running your own business

Writing a book

Planning a vacation

Planning a bank robbery

Staring into space

Staring at your computer screen to try to see each of the little dots individually

Transcendentally meditating

Taking an extended trip to the bathroom

Listening to a hypnotherapy tape to help you stop smoking

Listening to a hypnotherapy tape to help you lose weight

Listening to a hypnotherapy tape to help you conquer your addiction to hypnotherapy

Conducting a remote session with your personal therapist on the phone

Consulting your doctor on the phone

Talking with your interior decorator on the phone

Flirting with your lover on the phone

Asking a colleague to aid you in illicit behavior

Engaging in illicit behavior

Getting caught engaging in illicit behavior

Explaining why, in your view, the illicit behavior does not classify as gross misconduct

Deciding which days over the next year to take as sickies

Monitoring clouds

Learning how to forecast the weather by monitoring clouds

Monitoring pigeon-mating rituals

Monitoring the frequency of colleagues' bathroom breaks

Miscellaneous unproductive monitoring

Choosing a favorite mug

Looking at pictures of dogs dressed as bees

Looking at pictures of cats dressed as Harry Potter

Outrageous Expenses

"A billion here, a billion there—sooner or later it adds up to real money."

—*Senator Everett Dirksen*

AMONG the myriad annoyances within the office setting, expense claims are like an island paradise. Just when you're so irritated with the grinding tedium of yet another day at your desk, you remember that you haven't yet claimed back the money for your last cross-country meeting.

Most outrageous claims

An international survey found that almost 1 in 5 employees cheated employers by making extravagant expense claims, with the Americans and the French the most common culprits: 21.4 percent of American and 20.6 percent of French respondents admitted to fiddling their expenses, compared with 16.1 percent of Germans and 13 percent of British respondents.

What price pornography?

In the midst of the 2009 expenses scandal that rocked British Parliament, in which a variety of MPs were discovered to have expensed everything from duck islands to helipads, you almost had to feel for Home Secretary Jacqui Smith when it emerged that she had unwittingly claimed £5 (U.S. $8) for the cost of two pornographic films watched by her husband while she was trying to save the country from terrorists.

Apparently, she was left "mortified and furious" about the incident. She didn't seem to mind quite so much about the patio heaters or the kitchen sink that were also paid for out of her parliamentary expenses budget, however.

Business-critical buying

Members of the U.S. Congress face stricter rules about what they can claim on expenses, but it hasn't stopped them from doing their bit to compete with their British counterparts.

The *Wall Street Journal* recently investigated claims made on Capitol Hill and found the top three spenders were Representative Howard Berman, who charged $84,000 worth of personalized calendars, printed by the U.S. Capitol Historical Society, which he sent to his constituents; Representative Alcee Hastings, who stuck

$24,730 on the expense account for the lease of a 2008 luxury Lexus hybrid sedan; and Representative Michael Turner, who spent an extravagant $1,435 of taxpayers' money on a top-of-the-line digital camera. All of which were in accordance with congressional rules.

Preserving valuable artifacts

Outside the political field, taxpayers' cash is flashed in just as unseemly a way. In 2007, Lawrence Small, Secretary of the state-supported Smithsonian Institution in Washington, D.C., was found to have made claims amounting to $2 million in housing and office expenses over the previous six years.

The *Washington Post* uncovered spreadsheets and invoices for $15,000 for the replacement of French doors at Small's home and $48,000 for two chairs, a conference table, and the upholstery for his office suite. He also submitted receipts for $152,000 in utility bills, $273,000 in housekeeping services, and $203,000 in maintenance charges—including $2,535 to clean a chandelier.

On a smaller scale

Criticizing dubious claims by politicians is all very well, but international surveys show that the majority of us are more than willing to engage in, shall we say, *creative* expenses on a smaller scale.

The top 3 fake expense claims

1. Asking for extra taxi receipts and claiming false taxi transport
2. Adding extra mileage when submitting a claim
3. Using a cheap restaurant to entertain a client, then using an expensive restaurant for personal use and submitting the pricier receipt as expenses

> "Anyone who lives within their means suffers from a lack of imagination."
>
> —*Oscar Wilde*
>
> "More and more these days I find myself pondering how to reconcile my net income with my gross habits."
>
> —*John Nelson, musician*

Outrageous expenses claimed by real-life office workers

- A new motorcycle

- Vanity plate for a BMW

- Hiring a private investigator to find evidence to start divorce proceedings

- Lap dancers

- Viagra

- A goat

- A honeymoon

- Plastic surgery

- Hair extensions

- Charity donations

- Dancing lessons

- Twenty Bibles

A diamond ring

A haircut

A betting slip

A wardrobe of new clothes following a messy divorce

Vacations to Monte Carlo, Paris, and New York

Vet bill for neutering a cat

A pet hamster named Barry—for the office

Services rendered by a "lady of the night" while abroad

Pregnancy kit for a one-night stand

Collectible stamps for personal collection

Family trip to Disney World

New furniture for the house

Condoms

Getting away with it

If you've been caught trying to avoid paying your way, the honest thing to do is own up and cough up. Alternatively, you could follow the example of one daring young man faced with an unpaid chiropractor's bill.

From: Jane Gilles
Date: Wednesday 8 Oct 2008 12:19pm
To: David Thorne
Subject: Overdue account

Dear David,
Our records indicate that your account is overdue by the amount of $233.95. If you have already made this payment, please contact us within the next 7 days to confirm payment has been applied to your account and is no longer outstanding.

Yours sincerely, Jane Gilles

From: David Thorne
Date: Wednesday 8 Oct 2008 12:37pm
To: Jane Gilles
Subject: Re: Overdue account

Dear Jane,
I do not have any money so am sending you this drawing I did of a spider instead. I value the drawing at $233.95 so trust that this settles the matter.

Regards, David

From: Jane Gilles
Date: Thursday 9 Oct 2008 10:07am
To: David Thorne
Subject: Overdue account

Dear David,
Thank you for contacting us. Unfortunately we are unable to accept drawings as payment and your account remains in arrears of $233.95. Please contact us within the next 7 days to confirm payment has been applied to your account and is no longer outstanding.

Yours sincerely, Jane Gilles

From: David Thorne
Date: Thursday 9 Oct 2008 10:32am
To: Jane Gilles
Subject: Re: Overdue account

Dear Jane,
Can I have my drawing of a spider back then please.

Regards, David

From: Jane Gilles
Date: Thursday 9 Oct 2008 11:42am
To: David Thorne
Subject: Re: Re: Overdue account

Dear David,
You e-mailed the drawing to me. Do you want me to e-mail it back to you?

Yours sincerely, Jane Gilles

From: David Thorne
Date: Thursday 9 Oct 2008 11:56am
To: Jane Gilles
Subject: Re: Re: Re: Overdue account

Dear Jane,
Yes please.

Regards, David

From: Jane Gilles
Date: Thursday 9 Oct 2008 12:14pm
To: David Thorne
Subject: Re: Re: Re: Re: Overdue account

From: David Thorne
Date: Friday 10 Oct 2008 09.22am
To: Jane Gilles
Subject: Whose spider is that?

Dear Jane,
Are you sure this drawing of a spider is the one I sent you? This spider only has seven legs and I do not feel I would have made such an elementary mistake when I drew it.

Regards, David

From: Jane Gilles
Date: Friday 10 Oct 2008 11:03am
To: David Thorne
Subject: Re: Whose spider is that?

Dear David,
Yes it is the same drawing. I copied and pasted it from the e-mail you sent me on the 8th.

David your account is still overdue by the amount of $233.95. Please make this payment as soon as possible.

Yours sincerely, Jane Gilles

From: David Thorne
Date: Friday 10 Oct 2008 11:05am
To: Jane Gilles
Subject: Automated Out of Office Response

Thank you for contacting me.
I am currently away on leave, traveling through time and will be returning last week.

Regards, David

From: David Thorne
Date: Friday 10 Oct 2008 11:08am
To: Jane Gilles
Subject: Re: Re: Whose spider is that?

Hello, I am back and have read through your e-mails and accept that despite missing a leg, that drawing of a spider may indeed be the one I sent you. I realize with hindsight that it is possible you rejected the drawing of a spider due to this obvious limb omission but did not point it out in an effort to avoid hurting my feelings. As such, I am sending you a revised drawing with the correct number of legs as full payment for any amount outstanding. I trust this will bring the matter to a conclusion.

Regards, David

From: Jane Gilles
Date: Monday 13 Oct 2008 2:51pm
To: David Thorne
Subject: Re: Re: Re: Whose spider is that?

Dear David,
As I have stated, we do not accept drawings in lieu of money for accounts outstanding. We accept a check, bank check, money order, or cash. Please make a payment this week to avoid incurring any additional fees.

Yours sincerely, Jane Gilles

From: David Thorne
Date: Monday 13 Oct 2008 3:17pm
To: Jane Gilles
Subject: Re: Re: Re: Re: Whose spider is that?

I understand and will definitely make a payment this week if I remember. As you have not accepted my second drawing as payment, please return the drawing to me as soon as possible. It was silly of me to assume I could provide you with something of completely no value whatsoever, waste your time, and then attach such a large amount to it.

Bidding a Fond Farewell

"Please accept my resignation. I don't care
to belong to any club that will have me
as a member."

—*Groucho Marx*

SOONER or later every job comes to an end. Some unlucky ones are caught in a layoff, and others get promoted or simply retire. How dull. The lucky few are those who get the opportunity to resign in a blaze of bitter glory, leaving behind nothing but a dirty old mug, a few chewed pen tops, and, of course, the mother of all resignation letters.

As well as being incredibly cathartic, the resignation letter has the power to put a giant pin into that vast, straining balloon that is your boss's ego. If your experience has been tedious but relatively tolerable, damning with faint praise is the most satisfying sign-off, but if you've been waiting for this day for what feels like an eternity, then allow yourself to vent—better out than in, after all.

Incidentally, it's probably advisable to send your scathing letter at the last minute possible, since you may need to work out some sort of notice period under the person whose uselessness and bastardly ways you've just summarized in sonnet form.

Here are some examples of genuine resignation letters to give you some inspiration.

The Bitter

"I hope that I have had a positive influence and will be remembered favorably by those I have worked with, although I understand that, in reality, this is unlikely."

"For nearly as long as I've worked here, I've hoped that I might one day leave this company. And now that this dream has become a reality, please know that I could not have reached this goal without your unending lack of support. Words cannot express my gratitude for the words of gratitude you did not express."

"Your demands were high and your patience short, but I take great solace knowing that my work, as stated on my annual review, 'meets expectation.' That is the type of praise that sends a man home happy after a ten-hour day."

"In an age where miscommunication is all too common, you consistently impressed and inspired me with the sheer magnitude of your misinformation, ignorance and intolerance for true talent. It takes a strong man to admit his mistake—it takes a stronger man to attribute his mistake to me."

"I have been fortunate enough to work with some absolutely interchangeable supervisors on a wide variety of seemingly identical projects—an invaluable lesson in overcoming daily tedium in overcoming daily tedium in overcoming daily tedium."

"Over the past seven years you have taught me more than I could ever ask for and, in most cases, ever did ask for."

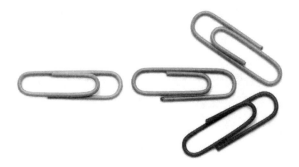

The Twisted

"In a world of managerial evolution, you are the blue-green algae that everyone else eats and laughs at."

"After many years of working waist deep in society's scum, I feel it is time to retire to greener pastures."

"I ask that you please accept my resignation as I cannot be part of an organization that would see fit to have me as a leader."

"In parting, if I could pass on any word of advice to the lower-salary recipient in India who will soon be filling my position, it would be to cherish this experience, because a job opportunity like this comes along only once in a lifetime. Meaning: If I had to work here again in this lifetime, I'd kill myself."

The Superior

"As a graduate of an institute of higher education, I have a few very basic expectations. Chief among these is that my direct superiors have an intellect that ranges above the common ground squirrel."

"In my time as your assistant, I've tried in vain to teach you how to print a document, how to select a font, how to work the drinks machine in the cafeteria and how to spell the word 'business.' I don't like to give up on a cause, but since I haven't seen any improvement over the past four years—and nobody's getting any younger here—I feel it is time for me to put my economics degree to better use elsewhere."

"Asking me to explain every little nuance of everything I do each time you happen to stroll into my office is not only a waste of time but also a waste of precious oxygen. I was hired because I know how to network computer systems; you were apparently hired to provide amusement to myself and other employees, who watch you vainly attempt to understand the concept of 'cut and paste' for the hundredth time. You will never understand computers. Something as incredibly simple as binary still gives you too many options."

The Superlative

"I pity you as a manager."

"As you probably know, today is my last day. But before I leave, I wanted to take this opportunity to let you know what a great and distinct pleasure it has been to type the words 'today is my last day.'"

"Managers like you are sad proof of the Dilbert Principle. Since this situation is unlikely to change without you getting a full frontal lobotomy reversal, I am forced to tender my resignation."

"I wish you had more of a backbone."

"After your consistent and annoying harassment of my coworkers and me during the commission of our duties, I can only surmise that you are one of the few true genetic wastes of our time."

"Try to use a spellcheck in your letter of reference, please; I hate having to correct your mistakes."

"I don't usually mix business with pleasure but today I'm going to make an exception—I resign."

How to Get Fired with Style

"I'm no fool. I've killed the boss. You think they're not going to fire me for a thing like that?"
—*Violet Newstead,* 9 to 5

THE one problem with a resignation, satisfying as writing that letter might be, is that there are usually rules attached. No matter how desperate you are to get out of there, if you play by the book, you will be bound by the terms of your pesky contract. It may be as long as three months before you're legitimately entitled not to show up at work, which seems almost like forced labor.

So if your heart simply isn't in it anymore and you decide you've got nothing to lose, a final showdown is guaranteed to get you fired in unforgettable style. But to get the full benefit of your immediate and uncontested freedom, you need to do something drastic. After all, if you're going to do something wrong, do it right.

Break the law

If you really want to go, this is the way to do it. It's the most surefire way to guarantee that you'll be given the boot. A burning-all-bridges no-going-back statement of intent. And I'm not talking about random acts of law-breaking here: The more specific you are, the better. You want to get fired from your job, so try to hone your crime to the issue at hand. Steal something from your boss, sabotage the company hard drive, crash your car into the emergency fire escape, or spray-paint somewhere prominent the words "I, [insert name], denounce you all as worshippers of the devil"—which, if you're lucky, will result in a charge of inciting religious hatred.

Ideally, time things so the police are actually called to the office and can escort you from the premises, allowing you to avoid all those tedious good-byes and disingenuous promises about keeping in touch.

Another entertaining option is to blackmail your boss, but bear in mind the possibility that your boss might have a lot of secrets that even you don't know about and might therefore go along with the blackmail rather than risk discovery. This would make the whole process very long-winded and would ultimately be a frustrating waste of time when all you wanted was an easy get-out clause.

Do nothing

It's amazing how tolerant employers can be when they think that someone is struggling with the most basic of life's tasks. Incompetence alone will simply not cut the mustard, and may, in fact, have the disastrous effect of turning you into your manager's pet project. It won't be long before you're being sent out of the office on special motivational days to keep your spirits up, or being offered talking computer equipment to help you succeed in the mainstream office environment. No, sadly for those who would rather just fail their way out of a job, it's just not that easy.

Point-blank refusal to lift a finger, however, will quickly do the trick. Try sitting with your feet up at your desk and taking a full hour to eat your lunch—if they try to interrupt you with an instruction, simply show them the flat of your hand and, with a full mouth, say, "Can't you see I'm eating?"

As long as they think you're trying, the guilt factor will be there, but the moment you demonstrate that you are both disrespectful and lazy, well, you'll be out of there in time to catch the lunchtime edition of *Columbo.*

Old-fashioned violence

Now don't go overboard on this one. A bit of squaring up and a few well-placed shadow kung-fu moves in the doorway to your boss's office should be more than adequate for your purposes. Violence at work—and that includes the threat of violence—constitutes gross misconduct, and that's the kind of term you need to be hearing if you want to get the heck out of there. It's definitely considered fair grounds for dismissal, although a careful employer might be more likely to ask you to take a period of unpaid leave until an official hearing can be arranged. If your aim is simply not to have to go back to that particular office ever again, this arrangement may well suit you best, since you can always claim in future interviews elsewhere that you were misunderstood.

Other forms of threatening behavior that you could pull off without actually hurting anyone include walking around the office with a voodoo doll of your boss and bandaging its mouth with tape in front of a crowd of (possibly appreciative) colleagues, or setting up a dartboard with your manager's face at the center.

Hitting the bottle

If all your surreptitious drinking has given you a taste for a regular snifter in the office, a small but public extension of your habit is grounds for dismissal in most companies. Check the rulebook carefully before you set about pickling your liver in your quest for freedom, though, and check out your company's track record. If precedents have been set by previous alcoholically inclined employees for the firm to support them on AA programs or similar, you may find yourself on an unwitting path to becoming a teetotaller. And, what's worse, still employed.

By far the safest method to use here is the out-and-out drunken one, where you show up at work completely inebriated for three days running. You can do it: just pretend you're at a music festival. The more vodka-fueled bad behavior you indulge in while you're under the influence, the better. Vomiting on the boss's shoes and having a nap on his desk are probably sackable offenses in their own right and will only help your cause.

Extracurricular activities

The ideal scenario here would be to have done something at some stage in your life that would get you fired if your employer found out about it. Forward-thinking employees who feel they may one day wish to get the sack quickly and easily with the minimum of effort should keep this in mind before they even enter the job market. An undisclosed criminal record will get you the boot with no questions asked—well, there may be *some* questions, such as why you withheld information about your convictions, but once you've spun them a few lies about feeling that you'd paid your debt to society, you'll be free to go.

If you have failed to secure any previous convictions about which to keep quiet, you could always generate some new ones. Or engage publicly in the kind of activities that would bring disrepute to your company—animal wrestling might work if you were employed by an animal-rights charity, for example, or eating in McDonald's if you work in PR for a vegan whole-foods supplier.

Be useless at your job

You need to be really and truly awful for this to work—a 10 on the scale of 1 to 10, where 1 is basically useless and 10 is record-breakingly incompetent. Strictly enforced employment laws may be partially to blame for the inordinate length of time it takes to get fired just by being moderately useless, but there could also be other factors at play. Perhaps your manager was also subpar when they started out and they can't help but take pity on their most incapable employees. Perhaps they know deep down that they're *still* useless now and are operating a policy of positive discrimination in an attempt to make themselves look better. Either way, simply being bad at your job is no way to go about soliciting a speedy sacking.

But if you're willing to play the long game, it could be an option worth considering. The main advantage is that, without a specific grievance against you, your employer won't be able to just give you the boot, but your utter uselessness will make them eager to see the back of you. This can, in rare and fortunate cases, result in the spectacularly pleasing arrangement of getting paid to leave. This differs from a layoff in that it's you personally, rather than your role, that is being ousted, but in the belief that you are desperate to hold on to your job, an employer will offer a cash consolation prize to ease the pain of leaving.

You can't lose.

Moonlighting

This requires a certain degree of effort that you may be loathe to undertake, given that you're plotting to get fired from the job you've already got, but give it a chance. The idea is to get another job for a rival firm without telling either employer about your double-dealing. Time management may be an issue, but with a bit of clever fiddling of the flex time and a few days' "sick leave" (see page 106), you should be able to pull it off for long enough to get fired from both jobs simultaneously.

The key to ensuring your dismissal in this case is to make sure you have betrayed each employer in some discernible way, ideally by revealing details of future product launches or next year's investment plans. This will throw up all sorts of exciting James Bond–style accusations, such as corporate spying and selling secrets, which should enhance your chances of getting a little of fresh air on your cheeks before the end of the week.

The Porn Ultimatum

A little bit of sensitivity is required with this one, since, according to the laws of most countries, viewing pornography at work is not strictly grounds for dismissal. It may be necessary, therefore, to get a rule banning the use of the Internet for downloading of pornography enshrined in your company's rulebook. If questions are asked later about why you so ardently championed a rule that you were about to break, you can add to your chances of dismissal by explaining that, for you, it was all part of the thrill.

If it is already against company rules and you can prove that you're a repeat offender, then justice should be swift.

Other easy ideas for a quick dismissal

Spend the day playing your favorite online game at your workstation. If caught, ask your boss if they'd like to face off.

Bring your pet to work. Encourage it to make itself at home in your manager's in-box.

Come to work with a two-week-old baby, if you can borrow one. Don't feel inhibited if you need to change its diaper on the counter in the staff kitchen.

Start a blog using your real name and talking about how bad the company you're working for is. When no one is looking, set it as the homepage for all computers.

Every morning, change the time on all the clocks in the office to 10 minutes before you clock out.

Write all-important documents backward or in another language. Chinese or Persian work well.

Sign up for multiple dating agencies using your boss's home phone number.

As soon as you make your first mistake, ask for a pay raise.

Wear a polka-dot clown suit to work. If asked to tone it down, come in the next day in flip-flops and shorts.

Impersonate your boss. Use a high-pitched voice for bonus points.

Photocopy your backside and pin it to the notice board.

Ask the chief executive for some rolling papers.

Tell the boss you'll "Send the boys around" if they don't authorize your pay raise.

Set up your own S&M dungeon in the supply closet.

Bring a sleeping bag to work for those little afternoon naps.

Pawn your work computer to cover you until payday.

Call the boss to your desk, address him as "Sonny," and tell him his work isn't up to scratch.

Wreaking Havoc As You Leave

"We should all do what in the long run gives us joy, even if it is only picking grapes or soiling the laundry.'

—*E. B. White*

AS soon as you know that you are actually going to be leaving the job that has sapped you of your *joie de vivre* for so long, it's as if a whole new world of possibilities opens up for you. I don't mean new job opportunities—no matter how pleased you are with whatever job you get next, the novelty will soon wear off—but the opportunities for laying waste to everything that you've spent the last few years of your life holding back the urge to destroy.

And in these dark days of economic woe, the majority of office workers faced with the possibility of dismissal admit that they don't plan on leaving empty-handed. A survey into the recession and its effects on work ethics questioned office workers and found that 60 percent would take valuable company data with them if they were asked to leave. In fact, 40 percent of them admitted that they had already begun downloading sensitive company secrets while their bosses' backs were turned, just in case they were fired.

Done. Now what?

But what if you want to go a step or two further and leave your mark on the company that has enslaved you for so long? Simply siphoning off material that they will also still be able to access doesn't feel quite dramatic enough. A veil has been lifted from your eyes, and for the first time you see how easy it would be. You're on your way out. This is your moment!

Delete all

Take a long last look at your computer screen, look at all those documents, those files full of information, the thousands of words that represent the blood, sweat, and tears that you spilled for your company, and now delete them all. Learn a lesson from the ancient Greeks: If you can't have it, burn it.

Become a lefty

It is important to write out instructions when passing the torch to a new hire or colleague, so in the guise of someone who is trying to give their final exit note a personal touch, write by hand. Most of us have become

Pink-Slipped Pilferers

Contact details of customers and clients are the most commonly pilfered items of information, but once you've plugged in the memory stick, it seems a waste to stop there—and most of us don't. Plans and proposals, detailed product information, and access and password codes all prove popular as mementoes.

What makes this cyber theft so easy is that memory sticks are not only small, cheap, and easy to use, they are one of the least traceable tools for downloading large amounts of data. Old-fashioned methods haven't been neglected altogether, though. Photocopying, e-mailing, downloading onto CDs, and using online encrypted–storage websites are all effective methods of making off with the company jewels. Camera phones, Skype recordings, and iPods also make useful receptacles for information. The smartest use a multitude of methods, burying small amounts of information in numerous different locations, like a squirrel burying nuts.

so accustomed to typing and texting that we have lost the power to grip a pencil. If you have somehow retained the long-lost art of writing, switch to your left hand so that it's definitely illegible.

Riddle me this

As a parting bit of office "fun," leave your replacement a series of riddles that, when solved, will reveal the logins and passwords that are essential for them to do their job. The more cryptic and infuriating they are, the better, so if you can do it letter by painstaking letter, you're onto a winner.

And Finally...

"Nothing is really work unless you would rather be doing something else."

—*J. M. Barrie*

WHEN you're having a particularly bad day at the office, when the new intern has spilled your coffee in your lap, when your boss is sending you an e-mail every five minutes demanding a new set of nasal-hair clippers and your office crush is flirting outrageously with your nemesis in Accounting, just remember that things are better than they used to be back in the day.

This notice overleaf dates from 1852 and sets out working conditions and rules to be observed by clerical staff who had just benefited from new labor laws.

1. Godliness, cleanliness, and punctuality are the necessities of good business.

2. The firm has reduced hours of work, and clerical staff will now only have to be present between the hours of 7:00 A.M. and 6:00 P.M. on weekdays.

3. Daily prayers will be held each morning in the main office; the clerical staff will be present.

4. Clothing must be worn of sober nature. The clerical staff will not disport themselves in raiment of bright colors, nor will they wear hose, unless in good repair.

5. Overshoes and topcoats may be worn in the office. Scarves and headgear may be worn in inclement weather.

6. A stove is provided for the benefit of the clerical staff; coal and wood must be kept in the locker. It is recommended that each member of the clerical staff brings four pounds of coal each day during cold weather.

7. No members of the staff may leave the room without permission from Mr. Rogers. The calls of nature are permitted without permission, and the clerical staff may use the garden below the second gate. This area must be kept in good order.

8. No talking is allowed during business hours.

9. The craving for tobacco, wine, or spirits is a human weakness and is forbidden to all members of the clerical staff.

10. Now that the hours have been drastically reduced, the partaking of food is allowed between 11:30 A.M. and noon, but work on no account ceases.

11. Members of the clerical staff will provide their own pens. A new sharpener is available on written application to Mr. Rogers.

12. Mr. Rogers will nominate a senior clerk to be responsible for the cleanliness of the main office and private office. All boys and juniors will report to him 40 minutes before prayers and will remain after closing hours for similar work. Brushes, brooms, scrubbing brushes and soap are provided by the management.

13. The new increased weekly wages are: junior boys to 11 years 1/4d; boys to 14 years 2/4d; juniors 4/8d; clerks 10/9d; senior clerks after 15 years service with the owner 21/-. The owners recognize the generosity of the new labor laws but will expect a great rise in output to compensate for these near utopian conditions.

"Be nice to nerds. Chances are you'll end up working for one."

—Bill Gates

Enjoy These Other Reader's Digest Best-Sellers

Make learning fun again with these light-hearted pages that are packed with important theories, phrases, and those long-forgotten "rules" you once learned in school.

$14.95 hardcover
ISBN 978–0–7621–0995–1

This laugh-out-loud collection of heartwarming examples of mistaken identity and senior moments, along with jokes, quips, truisms, and impish illustrations about the joys of aging, will keep you entertained for hours.

$14.95 hardcover
ISBN 978–1–60652–025–3

Starting to feel out of touch with the latest music? Does a night on the town leave you feeling exhausted? Then brace yourself: You might be middle-aged. This hilarious collection of midlife stories, quotes, and quips offers amusing insights into the other side of youth.

$14.95 hardcover
ISBN 978–1–60652–151–9

What makes "seventh heaven" and "cloud nine" so blissful and the number 13 so unlucky? Why is "555" the fake area code of Hollywood? This delightful book explores the role of numbers in expressions, novels, film, cultures, religion, and more.

$14.95 hardcover
ISBN 978–1–60652–134–2

A smorgasbord of foreign words and phrases used in everyday English—from Aficionado (Spanish) to Zeitgeist (German). Inside you'll find translations, definitions, and origins that will delight and amuse language lovers everywhere.

$14.95 hardcover
ISBN 978–1–60652–057–4

Reader's Digest books can be purchased through retail and online bookstores.
In the United States books are distributed by Penguin Group (USA), Inc.
For more information or to order books, call 1-800-788-6262.

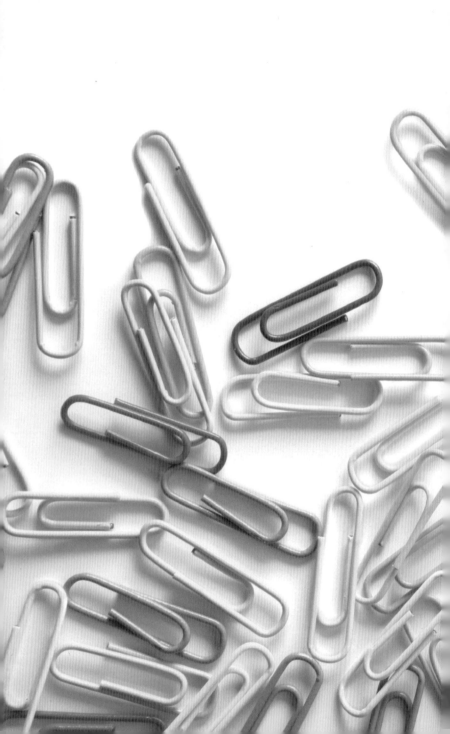